ALONGSIDE JESUS

Devotions for Teenagers

Drew Hill

New
Growth
Press

newgrowthpress.com

New Growth Press, Greensboro, NC 27401
newgrowthpress.com

Cover Design: Faceout Books, faceoutstudio.com
Interior Design and Typesetting: Gretchen Logterman

ISBN: 978-1-64507-248-5 (Print)
ISBN: 978-1-64507-249-2 (eBook)

Library of Congress Cataloging-in-Publication Data on file
LCCN 2022015955 (print) I LCCN 2022015956 (ebook)

Printed in the United States of America

29 28 27 26 25 24 23 22   1 2 3 4 5

Dedication

To our precious daughter, Honey.

You're my favorite teenager in the universe. I wrote these words so that you, your friends, and other teenagers you've never met would know Jesus. He loves you to death. Even more than I do. His love is perfect and everlasting. As you continue to grow in wisdom, and stature, and favor with God and man, I pray you will become even more aware of the nearness of Jesus. He's never been closer than he is right now. He is a God who walks alongside you every minute of every day. And he deeply delights in you. You're making him smile right now. You make me smile too. I'm so thankful I get to be your papa and walk through life alongside you.

- Dad

CONTENTS

Week 4

FOREWORD

Old Hillsboro Road was the curvy back road from work to home the summer after my senior year in high school. My world had been rocked from a traumatic experience, and my view of God was completely distorted. I felt numb and stuck with absolutely no idea of a solution for my pain or how to recover. I had been working so hard to earn God's approval and felt that it had all been in vain. Living in a house full of people, that twenty-minute drive was the only time I could turn off my pretending and let loose what was really going on in my heart. I would cry out at God, "Who are you really?! Who am I? Do you even love me?!"

My parents' friends and some peers in my life who sensed that I was really struggling would often tell me to "remind myself of my identity in Christ." They meant well, but because I was in such a rough place with God, it just sounded fluffy and disconnected from my personal story. "You are a child of God, bought with a price," they would say, and I thought, *If everybody has this same identity, then am I not unique and special? And does God not really love me for me?* It felt almost like I had to pursue God when I really wanted him to pursue me. I hate to say it, but this advice ended up pushing me even further away.

On a particularly discouraging day on Old Hillsboro Road, I felt like I could hear God's voice breaking through the silence, asking "Franni, what do you like?" I thought to myself, *If you're God, don't you already know?* But I started throwing things out there. "I like jazz on the beach, being barefoot, feeling like someone is really listening to me when I'm sharing my heart, being able to sing from my soul, feeling totally and completely free, letting out a good cry, swimming uncomfortably far out in the ocean, and PB&J sandwiches."

For the first time in a long time, I could almost see the pure joy in a smile on God's face as he took a step back to look at me and say, "Franni, I like you." The encounter struck me right in the core of my being and stopped me in my tracks. "I like you" in that moment felt like an even bigger deal than "I love you." He likes me for me and all of the unique things about me. God doesn't just love me because he has to.

My experience that day hammered a huge crack in the wall between God and me. The foundation of my faith began to be rebuilt. I learned (and am still learning) that walking with God is about living *from* his love rather than *for* his love. This transformation can only come through personal encounters with the living God, where he speaks life and healing into our hearts.

The teenage years can be one of the most difficult times in a person's life. There are so many conflicts of identity and attacks against the soul. *Alongside Jesus* is an incredible tool that does an amazing job of sparking these sacred, vital encounters with the living God. The questions, the prompts, and the stories in this book all soften the heart and prepare the reader to meet with Jesus and hear from him for themselves.

Thank you, Drew, for following God's call to write this wonderful book. I am so excited for all of the many people that are going to experience freedom as they fall into the arms of their loving Savior as they read the words on these pages.

Franni Rae Cash Cain, We the Kingdom

Man, I wish I had had this book when I was in high school. This season can be such a scary time, and I remember often feeling alone—even and especially in a crowd. I could be surrounded by people but feeling like I was the only one who felt the way I did, and that no one else could really see me and relate to all I was going through. I thought of God as this far-off being that didn't want anything to do with me and wasn't interested in my personal life. Nothing could be further from the truth!

This book is an amazing tool as it uses the Word of God to show how Jesus wasn't just some long-haired hippie that lived a long, long time ago, but that he is very much alive and wants to walk with us throughout life. Who better to show us how to live than the Creator of life itself! I see now I'm not alone, that Jesus is with me. Alongside me. And that is awesome.

Ed Cash, We the Kingdom

INTRODUCTION

"They were in the midst of a discussion about all the events of the last few days when Jesus walked up and accompanied them in their journey. **They were unaware that it was actually Jesus walking alongside them**. . . ." Luke 24:14–16a (TPT)

Have you ever considered that Jesus could actually be walking alongside you?

Like right now. In this very moment. Even though you can't see him.

If that were true, how would it change your day? Your life?

Use your imagination for a moment. The door to your room slowly opens. Like a surprise appearance from a close friend, Jesus swings around the corner, face painted with excitement. Your heart rate skyrockets. Your stomach drops. You're overcome with emotion. Before you know it, he's lifting you up in a bear hug. You recognize his scent. You feel his heart beat against yours. Then he sets you down and slowly takes a step back. His eyes meet yours. He cups your head in his nail-scarred hands and looks deeper into your eyes than anyone has in such a long, long time. With unquestionable delight, Jesus says _____. He calls you by name.

It seems like sometime between ages nine and twelve, there's an unspoken rule that kids are supposed to grow out of their imagination. You're no longer supposed to believe in the tooth fairy or the bogeyman. You don't take pictures with

Disney princesses or the Chick-fil-A cow anymore. So, at first, it can feel silly and childish to try and use your imagination. But in reality, teenagers actually use their imaginations a lot, maybe even more than children.

Think about it. Have you ever scanned through mental images of the kind of car you want to drive some day? Or day-dreamed about someone? Or envisioned hitting a last-second-game-winning shot? Have you ever watched a suspenseful movie and been unable to go to sleep afterward? Have you replayed scenes from your school day over and over in your mind—sometimes rewriting the script? Have you ever read a fantasy novel or played a video game and gotten so wrapped up in the make-believe that it actually felt real? Isn't it crazy how reading words on a page or pressing buttons on a controller can make your heart feel like you're running a race?

My friend John once asked the question, "Did God give us an imagination just so we can play pretend, or could it possibly be a gift that helps us grow closer to Jesus?"[1]

I like watching YouTube clips of behind-the-scenes footage from movies. The green-screen scenes, the costume designs, the bloopers, and outtakes. But when I go into the theatre, I'm thankful for the hours of video editing that produced a final product that allows our imaginations to explode.

I hope the words in these pages strike a match that ignites an explosion in you—a firework's display in your imagination. The goal of this book is not just to download more information about Jesus into your brain. It's much bigger. I want you to actually encounter him. To interact with him. To hear him call *your* name. I want you to know you're never alone and that Jesus actually walks alongside you every single second of every single day. And that he's with you right now.

It first clicked for me one summer when I was thirteen. There are still lots of days when I forget that Jesus is walking alongside me. But you know what? The more I get to know him, the quicker I remember he's there. Jesus has changed my life and I can't wait to tell you how amazing he is.

Over this next month, we're going to look at different things Jesus does when he's walking alongside you. Jesus shows, asks, listens, sees, moves, rests, prays, walks, understands, calms, corrects, redefines, hates, forgives, rejoices, and wants.

Near the end of the gospel of John, the author shares the purpose of his writing.

"These [stories] are written so that you may believe that Jesus is the Messiah, the Son of God, and that by believing you may have life in His name" (John 20:31).

That's the same reason I wrote this book for you. So that your faith in Jesus would grow and that by believing in him, you may experience life to the full.

Alongside you,

FIVE THINGS YOU NEED

DON'T SKIP OVER THIS SECTION! In order to have the full "Alongside" experience, you're going to need a few additional things to go along with this book.

1. A BIBLE

Choose a translation that's easy for you to understand.

Word-for-word translations include:

- NASB (New American Standard Bible)
- ESV (English Standard Version)
- KJV (King James Version)
- NKJV) (New King James Version)

Paraphrase translations include:

- MSG (The Message)
- CEV (Contemporary English Version)
- NIRV (New International Reader's Version)
- PHILLIPS (JB Phillips New Testament)
- Da Jesus Book (Hawaiian Pidgin New Testament)

Meet-in-the-middle translations include:

- NIV (New International Version)
- CSB (Christian Standard Bible)
- NLT (New Living Translation)

If you have trouble finding the Scripture passages, use the Table of Contents in the front of your Bible to locate the book. The Bible is actually made up of sixty-six smaller books. Most of the passages I write about are found in the New Testament, which is the back half of the Bible, and it contains twenty-seven books. A large majority of the Scripture passages in this book are found in the Gospels, which are Matthew, Mark, Luke, and John—the first four books in the New Testament. The first part of the Bible, the Old Testament, was written before Jesus came as a baby, and it contains thirty-nine books. Each of the sixty-six books of the Bible are divided up by chapter numbers, and each chapter has verses. So, if you see something like John 5:1–14, that means the passage is found in the book of John (fourth book in the New Testament), in the fifth chapter of that book, and in the first fourteen verses.

2. A PEN

I know some people do not like writing in their Bible or books, but **DO IT ANYWAY**! A big part of this book is being willing to engage with it, and not just read it. A helpful way to do that is by actually circling words, underlining sentences, jotting down questions, and even drawing a picture every now and then. It's also helpful to read your Bible with a pen in hand. I still have my Bible from high school filled with questions, notes, and highlights.

3. A QUIET PLACE

The world is full of distractions. Even if you're in your own room, I imagine there are lots of distractions. Before you dive into *Alongside Jesus* each day, I'd encourage you to create as much of a **DISTRACTION-FREE ENVIRONMENT** as possible. Maybe that means turning on some white noise—like a fan or sound machine—so you can't hear your little brother playing his drums. Maybe that means turning off any screens or devices that are tempting you to look at them.

4. A Slower Pace

Lots of devotionals are shorter and can be read and checked off your to-do list in minutes. These devotions are intentionally designed to take longer. I'm grateful for fast-food, but there's something special about sitting down to a home-cooked meal and chewing slowly. The goal isn't just to devour these pages, it's to encounter the person of Jesus. How do you get to know someone deeply? By reading their social media posts, or by taking a walk with them?

You're officially invited to **WALK** through this book. Please **DON'T RUN**. Each seven-day week is set up with only four devos. This allows you to miss a couple of days and not get behind. If you find it annoying to not have one to do every day, on day five or six you could reread some of the biblical passages from that week and see how Jesus meets you differently when you go back for seconds. The point is to go slow. This isn't a race; this is a relationship.

One helpful practice is picking a specific time each day to engage with this book and God's Word. We walk alongside Jesus all day long, but it's helpful to actually schedule when you are going to carve out time to read and do these exercises. Most of these devos will take you somewhere between twenty to thirty minutes. When would that work best in your rhythm of life?

If possible, I would encourage you to do it first thing in the morning to set the tone for your day. But if you're not a morning person and that sounds like torture, consider doing it as the last thing before you go to sleep each night. That might mean giving up some screen time, but my guess is that spending time with Jesus will allow you to experience a deeper rest than anything you'll see on your screen. But show yourself some grace too. It's OK to miss a day!

Sample Schedule (create one that works for you):

Monday - Day 1

Tuesday - Day 2

Wednesday- Whoops, I overslept! That's OK, I can do it tonight or tomorrow.

Thurs - Day 3

Friday - Day 4

Saturday - Resting today

Sunday - Weekend conversation with my Alongsider

5. An Alongsider

It might feel intimidating, but trust me on this. Muster up the courage and ask someone to go through this book *alongside* you. Maybe that's a friend, parent, grandparent, youth leader, coach, teacher, pastor, Young Life leader, or a sibling. When you commit to reading it together, it gives you someone to process it with. Consider this: If a friend asked you to do a devo with them for a month, how would you feel? See, you'd be honored! **BE BRAVE** and **INVITE SOMEONE** into this journey alongside you. You'll be thankful you did.

After every four days, you'll find a section called "The Weekend Conversation." This is a set of questions for you to talk through with your Alongsider. You'll be tempted to skip it and just move on to the next day. Fight that temptation. Call your devo-partner (or better yet, take a **WEEKEND WALK** together) and spend some time reflecting on the past week. My guess is that it will end up being your favorite part of this whole thing.

WEEK 1

DAY 1: JESUS SHOWS

"The Son is the image of the invisible God, the firstborn over all creation." (Colossians 1:15)

QUESTION

When you picture the face of God, what do you see?

What facial expression is he making when he looks at you? And how is it even possible for us to know if what we're imagining is true?

I love comparing baby pictures of my kids to my own baby pictures. I feel a good sense of pride when people see the resemblance. I imagine that's how God, the Father, feels about his Son, Jesus.

SCRIPTURE

All throughout Scripture, it's clear that Jesus is the visible expression of the invisible God.

The apostle Paul writes, "We look at this Son and see the God who cannot be seen" (Colossians 1:15 MSG). Another translation puts it this way: "He is the divine portrait, the true likeness of the invisible God . . ." (Colossians 1:15a TPT).

In John 1:14, John writes, "The Word became flesh and made his dwelling among us. We have seen his glory, the glory of the one and only Son, who came from the Father, full of grace and truth."

In John 10:30, Jesus himself tells us, "I and the Father are one.'"

Jesus shows us the face of God.

STORY

I remember going to summer camp right before eighth grade. That was the year I started asking more questions about God.

Each night, the camp speaker opened the Gospels and shared stories about Jesus. He told us how getting to know Jesus helps us get to know God. Then, he told us how much Jesus loved us. This frustrated me. Mid-week, I cornered the speaker after his talk and said, "Chris, you're being really repetitive. We know Jesus loves us. We get it! You can move on. Tell us how we're supposed to be better people and stuff. You don't have to keep harping on his love. Tell us what we need to do."

With kindness in his eyes, he leaned against the stage and listened. Then he slowly replied, "Drew, I'm not sure you do get it. When Jesus's love grabs hold of you, that is what changes you—not a list of ways to be a better person."

I had grown up in the church, heard about Jesus, and called myself a Christian for years, but that was the first time someone had ever made me question if I truly understood Jesus's love for me. At that moment, I felt incredibly lost.

On the first day of that week, everyone was placed on a team. At the week's end, the winning team was awarded the cherished "Camp Champ" t-shirts. Points were distributed for winning competitions, memorizing verses, and performing obnoxious team cheers. There were bonus points for anyone who got up before breakfast and walked around the lake. I wasn't a morning person, but I loved winning, so I decided I would wake up early every morning and help my team take home the shirts.

It was about a half mile around the lake, and you got points for each lap, but the rule was you had to walk, not run. And you had to walk by yourself. And you had to be silent. As an extrovert, I'd never intentionally spent that much time alone or in silence. This camp was nestled in the North Carolina mountains and most mornings there was a mist that fell heavy on the lake. Often the fog was so thick that I couldn't see ten feet in front of me. During those mornings I began talking and listening to Jesus in a way I never had before.

Jesus

The morning after that conversation with Chris, I had a conversation with Jesus. We talked while we walked.

"Jesus, I've been trying to live 'the Christian life' for a long while, and to me, it feels a lot like this competition at camp. The more I behave, the better I perform, the more likely I am to win at this religion thing. The more likely I am to be liked. But after this week, and Chris's talks, I'm thinking I might be getting the whole thing wrong. I want to understand your love for me, but I honestly don't know what to do. Jesus, will you help me?"

I didn't hear an audible response from him, but that morning, during the final lap around the lake, I experienced Jesus's presence walking alongside me. I don't really know how to describe it. All I know is that he answered my prayer and gave me faith to believe that he was with me.

A big part of being a teenager is asking questions. My guess is that, much like teenage Drew, you probably wonder what God is like, if he's real, and how he feels about you.

In the person of Jesus, we get answers to those questions. Jesus Christ reveals God's heart to us.

Since none of us were alive 2,000 years ago when Jesus walked the earth, how do we know what Jesus was like? The same way we know what our great grandparents were like. We listen to stories.

You're holding a book full of stories. True stories.

Stories about a man named Jesus.

Stories about my friends who are your age.

And hopefully, you'll read some stories about you.

As you read the stories of Jesus that show us what God is like, read them with your mind, because these stories are true. The gospel accounts are factual, historical reports. They were recorded by people who either knew Jesus firsthand, or by close companions of people who were eyewitnesses of the risen Christ.

But don't just read them like a textbook. These tales are much more like love stories and action movies. Let your heart get wrapped up in the wonder of God's love for you. Try to imagine what it might have felt like to be there 2,000 years ago. In the very presence of Jesus. God with skin on.

Imagine being at the wedding when he turned water into wine, or in the boat when he calmed the raging storm. When you put yourself in the scene, what do you see? What do you see on the face of Jesus? What do you hear, smell, taste and feel?

In the classic French novel, *Les Misérables*, Victor Hugo wrote, "Le suprême bonheur de la vie, c'est la conviction qu'on est aimé ; aimé pour soi-même, disons mieux, aimé malgré soi-même."[2]

The English translation is, "The greatest happiness of life is the conviction that we are loved; loved for ourselves, or rather, loved in spite of ourselves."

God has communicated his love for us in dozens of ways. He reveals it in sunsets, friendships, taste buds, and songs. But if you've ever doubted the way God feels about you, there's nothing more convincing than the person of Jesus. And I am convinced that if you truly get to know him, you can't help but fall in love with him.

TODAY'S ALONGSIDE PRACTICE

We live in a ridiculously fast-paced culture. You might be tempted to read each day's devotion pretty quickly, check it off your to-do list, and then move on with the rest of your day. But getting to know Jesus is more like walking than running.

So, in order to help you slow down and move beyond the reading, at the end of each devotion, you'll find a simple practice. Imagine being in a school play, or performing a recital, or competing in a big game—without ever practicing. Imagine marrying someone without ever going on a date.

The practices offered at the end of each devo are designed to help you get to know Jesus. Some of them will be easier than others. Some of them will be super short, like this one below. Others will take a little more time and intentionality. Some of them will take courage. All of them are designed to help you become more aware that Jesus is actually alongside you.

This first one is easy. Simply draw a vertical line between the *w* and the *h* in the sentence at the top of the next page.

Then rewrite the sentence by replacing that vertical line with a space. Then strike through the original. Consider writing that new sentence on a notecard and putting it on the wall by your bed. Or grab a dry erase marker and write it on your mirror.

GOD IS NOWHERE.

Each day, I'll suggest a song for you to listen to that goes along with the devo. Here's the first one:

SONG

"More Like Love" by Ben Rector

DAY 2: JESUS ASKS

"Turning around, Jesus saw them following and asked, 'What do you want?'" (John 1:38)

Question

Do you know the first words Jesus speaks in the gospel of John?

You cheated and looked at the verse above, didn't you? Well, you answered correctly. He asked a question: **"What do you want?"**

When you picture God, do you picture someone who is asking questions? Or do you picture someone who is giving a lecture? If Jesus shows us what God is like, it's worth paying attention to the fact that he asks over 100 questions while interacting with people in the Gospels. That's a lot of questions! It's crazy to think that the God, who created the world—a world currently populated with **8 BILLION DIFFERENT PEOPLE**—takes time to ask personal questions to individual people.

Scripture

Take a minute and open your Bible and read John 5:1–9. Seriously. Don't skip this part. Underline in your Bible any words or phrases that stick out to you.

(BIBLE READING BREAK . . .)

Alright, now reread it, and this time, use your imagination. Visualize what it might have been like if you were actually there, and you were paralyzed too, and you were lying ten feet from the paralyzed man. How bad does it smell? Are bugs crawling on you? What sounds do you hear around you? Are people moaning in pain? What does Jesus's voice sound like? Do you believe that Jesus is actually going to heal this man? And if so, could he heal you too?

As you read through this devotional, I'll often prompt you to write down at least THREE WONDERINGS: Three things that you wonder about as you read the Scriptures. I personally find this to be such a helpful way for me to engage with the Bible, and I hope it will be for you as well. For this first exercise, I'm going to write down some of my own wonderings that popped into my head as I read John 5. After you read mine, write down three of your own below it.

I know that might seem annoying, but trust me, it's worth writing them down. God wired our brains and bodies in a way that we actually experience gradual transformation when we physically participate in simple practices like this.

DREW'S WONDERINGS:

- What is the man's name?

- How did he get paralyzed thirty-eight years ago? Was he born like that? Did he get beat up by a bully? Did he have an accident?

- Where is his family? Did they abandon him? Does he have any friends? Is he completely alone?

My Wonderings:

- I wonder…

- I wonder…

- I wonder…

John tells us in the first verse of chapter 5 that Jesus was there for a feast. It was Passover week in Jerusalem. Every Jewish family from miles around had traveled up the mountain for the greatest celebration of the year. During the festival, hundreds of thousands of visitors would flood into the city. It was a claustrophobic person's nightmare. If you've ever been in line for the bathroom during intermission at a big concert or halftime at a sporting event, you can envision the crowd.

But it wasn't just people clogging the streets. Many of the travelers had brought lambs that would soon be sold and slaughtered for the Passover meal. There were five gates used to enter the walled city, and one of them was called the Sheep Gate. Through that gate walked a parade of three hundred thousand sheep. Imagine what it smelled like! The stench of the sun beating down on animal dung. This wasn't the VIP entrance. But this was the gate Jesus chose.

And next to the gate was a pool. It was believed that when God stirred the pool, the first one in the water would be healed. That's the background of the conversation you just eavesdropped in on—a conversation between Jesus and a man who hadn't walked in thirty-eight years.

In verse 6, John writes, "When Jesus saw him lying there and learned that he had been in this condition for a long time, he asked him, 'Do you want to get well?'" If you overheard the interaction, you might at first assume that Jesus was mocking the man. How insensitive to even ask that question. Of course the man would love to get well, wouldn't he?

STORY

One night I was eating dinner with my friend Russ. He's twenty-four years old. It was six o'clock and he'd just gotten out of bed for the first time that day. We'd gotten together at his request, so I started the conversation with a simple question: "What's on your mind?"

Russ looked me right in the eyes and said, "Man, I'm just tired of the way I'm living. I party or play video games all night long. I sleep all day. I've wrecked three cars. I've lost my license. My job sucks. My roommates are idiots. And I feel like I'm a disappointment to everyone around me, especially to my parents."

I responded with a couple more questions. "How tired are you? Are you tired enough to make some changes?"

Russ looked at the ground. "I don't know, man. I don't know."

I told him I'd love to help him start a new path, and I offered him some options. I haven't heard from him since.

JESUS

Sometimes we get so comfortable in our routines that, even when we have the chance to get well, we'd rather just stay right where we are. When talking to the invalid by the Sheep Gate, Jesus was asking him an honest question: "Are you set in your ways, or would you like to know what it's like to have legs that can walk?"

John 5:7–8 shows us his response: "'Sir,' the invalid replied, 'I have no one to help me into the pool when the water is stirred. While I am trying to get in, someone else goes down ahead of me.'"

He sounds a lot like my friend Russ. Lots of excuses. Glass half empty. Little hope of things ever changing. I wonder if there were additional parts of their conversation John didn't record—or if Jesus just jumped right in with a mind-blowing display of grace and power. "Then Jesus said to him, 'Get up! Pick up your mat and walk.' At once the man was cured; he picked up his mat and walked" (vv. 8–9).

Maybe Jesus healed everyone who was there by the pool that day. Or maybe just that one guy. But for some reason, the disciple John recorded this conversation between a sick man and the healing Messiah. And John shows us a clear picture of God's heart. A God who didn't just put on skin and come to earth to cure us, but to actually interact with us, to ask us questions, and to know our deepest desires.

Jesus didn't arrive shouting rebukes and commands. He simply asked a question: "Do you want to get well?"

It's just day two of this devotional, but I would pose the same question to you? Do YOU want to get well?

Are you content with the way things are? If so, go ahead and donate this devo to your local Goodwill. But if you want to be healed, the first step in knowing the Healer is admitting you're sick.

Today's Alongside Practice

Spend some time answering Jesus's two questions from today:

"What do you want?" and *"Do you want to get well?"*

You can whisper your answers aloud in your room.

You can take a walk in your neighborhood and pray them aloud.

You can write them down on this page and hide your book under your mattress.

Maybe you share your need with Jesus through one of the prayers below:

(Star the prayers that you can relate to)

❐ Jesus, I am overwhelmed with worry. It feels like I can't control my thoughts. Why do I always imagine worst-case-scenarios? My mind and heart constantly race. Every day feels like a battle to just breathe. Heal me of my anxiety.

❐ Jesus, I get so annoyed with my parents and siblings. I have little patience with my teachers, coaches and peers. Why won't people just leave me alone?! Jesus, please heal me of my anger.

☐ Jesus, I hate the way I look. Why do others have it so much easier than me. Comparison steals my joy. I feel like I'm never enough. Never good enough. Pretty enough. Smart enough. Athletic enough. Cool enough. Heal me of my envy and insecurity.

☐ Jesus, I live so much of my life in secret. If people knew what I did behind closed doors, they would surely reject me. Can I ever be honest about my struggles? Would anyone love me if they knew the truth about me? Heal me of my addictions and deceit.

☐ Jesus, I have zero motivation to do anything that matters. I feel like my life has no purpose. What am I even doing here? Heal me of my apathy.

☐ Jesus, I feel like such a fake. I act one way in front of adults and a completely opposite way in front of my friends. Who I am on social media is a masquerade. It's not who I really am. Heal me of my hypocrisy.

☐ Jesus, I am so thankful I don't have anxiety, anger, insecurity, addictions, apathy or pretend to be someone I'm not. I'm so much better off than my peers. They all have so many problems, but not me! I am always unselfish, humble, and confident. OK, maybe not always. OK, maybe I need healing too. Would you heal me of my judgmental spirit?

☐ Jesus, I need to be the center of attention. I need to be liked. I need to be noticed. Heal me of my need for approval.

☐ Jesus, I don't want to do this silly exercise. I don't even want to talk to you. I'm not even sure you're real. But if you are, would you heal me of my unbelief?

SONG

"SOS" by We the Kingdom

DAY 3: JESUS LISTENS

"Then the woman, scared and shaking all over . . . came and flung herself before [Jesus] and **told him the whole story**" (Mark 5:33 PHILLIPS).

QUESTION

Yesterday, you had an opportunity to answer Jesus's questions. Maybe you dug deep and found the courage to confess your need of healing. If so, way to go! If not, it's never too late to have that conversation. But a hard part of talking to someone you can't see, is wondering if they're actually listening. If God is busy running the universe, does he really have time to hear about my little problems?

In today's encounter, we get the answer to that question. Remember, Jesus shows us God's heart, so when we watch how Jesus interacts with the bleeding woman, we can know with confidence that he cares for us in much the same way.

SCRIPTURE

Just like yesterday, grab your Bible and a pen. Slowly read Mark 5:21–34 and imagine yourself in the story.

My Wonderings:

• How did the woman hear about Jesus? Who told her?

• I wonder…

• I wonder…

• I wonder…

At the beginning of this passage, it feels like Jesus is walking curiously slow. Shouldn't he be running? It's an emergency! A little girl is dying! And then, to delay things even more, he gets interrupted by someone else who needs him. To Jairus, the synagogue ruler and dad of the dying daughter, it must have felt maddening. It was like his little girl's ambulance driver got detoured in the parade of people. For a moment, he had Jesus's sole attention, but everyone was longing to get close to the healer. Especially this woman who had been hemorrhaging for twelve years.

And as soon as she touched Jesus's clothes, her bleeding stopped. But that's not even the most amazing part of the story. Everyone already knew that the God-man had the power to heal. The show-stopper is that in the midst of the crowd, chaos, and cries of a desperate father, Jesus stops and looks around. He's not ruled by the anxiety of the moment. He's not rushing anywhere. He is watching and listening. He is offering his presence and peace.

> At once Jesus knew intuitively that power had gone out of him, and he turned around in the middle of the crowd and said, 'Who touched my clothes?' His disciples replied, 'You can see this crowd jostling you. How can you ask, "Who touched me?"' **But he looked all around at their faces to see who had done so.** (Mark 5:30–32 PHILLIPS)

Can you picture the scene? The sea of people pressing in, all wanting a moment with the Messiah. Arms and hands reaching for him. After he felt the power go out of him, Jesus stops, gets on his tip-toes and, scans the crowd. "He looked all around at their faces to see who had [touched him]" (v. 32).

That's when their eyes met. Until that moment, she'd only seen him from behind. She'd only brushed her hand across the back of his robe. But now, she saw the face of God. His eyes invited her closer.

> And scared and shaking all over . . . she came and flung herself before him and told him the whole story. (v. 33)

Have you ever flung yourself at anyone's feet? Have you ever been so desperate for help that you couldn't even stand up? Have you ever been able to share all the details of your messy story with someone else?

Over the years, I've had the holy privilege of being in many of those conversations with my teenage friends. Through tears, they've shared about broken relationships with parents, painful rejection from friends, secret addictions, and guilty regrets. If you've never been able to be honest with anyone about your own pain, Jesus longs to listen to you, just like he did with the bleeding woman. (In case you're also wondering if Jesus also listened to Jairus and his daughter, read the rest of the story in Mark 5:35–43.)

Knowing Jesus, I imagine after the woman flung herself at his feet, he knelt down beside her, maybe even holding her hands in his. She must have been so weary, so desperate, so hopeless.

Jesus was genuinely interested in hearing her whole story. I wonder where she started. Did she rewind back to the beginning? Did she tell him about her life twelve years ago, before the bleeding began? How long did they sit there and chat?

After she had finished telling him her whole story, look how Jesus responded. In addition to healing her body, the Great Physician used the power of his words to restore her very soul. "He said to her, 'Daughter, it is your faith that has healed you. Go home in peace, and be free from your trouble'" (v. 34).

This is the only time in all of the Gospels when we hear Jesus call someone DAUGHTER.

Then, he calls her courageous. Can you hear his kind voice? "My daughter, you are so brave. You had every reason to give up the fight. And yet, against all odds, you persevered. Instead of bitterness, your heart is filled with hope and faith. And that courageous faith has healed you. Be encouraged. You are one of a kind. And you are loved. Go live in freedom."

She likely entered the crowd anonymously, ashamed, with her head hung low. I'd imagine she left feeling heard, loved, and fully accepted.

STORY

For the past twenty years, almost every summer I've taken some teenage friends on a backpacking trip. On the first of these adventures, our guides for the week started a tradition that has continued each year.. At the beginning of the hike, they passed around a bag of M&M's. Each camper took a few, leaving enough so the bag could make it all the way around the circle. Once the M&M's were divvied out, the guides asked everyone to count and then report how many they took. The guides then shared that over the course of the week, while stopping for meals on the trail, each person would get a chance to share one **MEMORY** or **MILESTONE**—one M&M—for each of the M&M's taken from the bag. Over the course of the next six days, each of us was gifted an hour to share about any memories and milestones that had shaped our lives. It was powerful to watch others let their guards down and take off their masks. Part of being human is longing to be known.

I recently read my journal from a trip we took a few years ago. I'd written down notes on what some of the guys had shared. Underneath my friend Sean's name, four things were written.

Sean's Memories and Milestones

- The times I've made my mom cry
- The year my dad coached my team and was proud of me
- When only one friend showed up at my eighth-grade birthday party
- When I got hurt my junior year and couldn't play ball

What a gift it is to get a front-row seat as another person pulls the cover off their heart and hesitantly, but bravely, shows it off—in all its mess and glory. In those holy moments, strangers somehow become siblings.

Jesus

Isn't that what we all long for? To be listened to and loved? To be treated like family?

After Jesus listened to the bleeding woman's story, he called her "daughter." He made sure she knew that she wasn't rejected, but that she absolutely belonged.

Jesus wants to call you his child, too.

Today's Alongside Practice

As you long to belong, below are two practical ways you can encounter the presence of Jesus.

Both require a similar courage of "the bleeding daughter" and my friend Sean.

1. Think about the adults in your life who remind you of Jesus. Do you know their stories? Do you know what their teenage years were like? Do you know how they started walking alongside Jesus? Pick one or two of them and reach out to them today. Maybe it's your Alongsider. Maybe it's a parent or a teacher or a youth leader. Send them a message like this:

Hey _____ (write their name here; it'll help motivate you to actually contact them),

I read this devo today and it talked about how Jesus listens to our whole stories. I was wondering if you had any time this week to get together? I realize that I've actually never heard your whole story, and I'd love to know more about what you were like when you were my age and how you started walking with Jesus. If you're up for that, let me know a time that works for you. Thanks!

2. After they share their story with you, ask if you could share a few of your M&M's with them. Spend some time right now listing memories and milestones that have shaped you into the person you are today. List both the hard things and the good things. Before you share them with another person, share them with Jesus. As you reflect back over your own story, thank him for the blessings and tell him how you truly feel about the painful memories. He longs to listen to your whole story.

Below is another example list from a friend of mine who is a senior in high school:

- When my neighbor passed away
- When I lost my innocence through peer pressure
- When I went to summer camp and realized that God is not only real, but also good
- When my dad still loved me after I messed up big time
- When I was rejected by my dream college

My M&M's:

-

-

-

-

-

-

SONG

"I am Your Beloved" by Jonathan David and Melissa Helser

DAY 4: JESUS SEES

"When Jesus reached the spot, **he looked up and saw the man** and said, 'Zacchaeus, hurry up and come down. I must be your guest today.'" (Luke 19:5 PHILLIPS)

QUESTION

Who is the most popular cultural icon among your peers? A musician? An athlete? A social media influencer? Picture that person walking into the halls of your school tomorrow. What would happen? Would they get swarmed by students for selfies?

That's what it was like for Jesus. His public appearances turned into pop-up parades. And just like the story of the "bleeding daughter," today's account centers around another person who longed to get close to Jesus. But he had to figure out how to navigate the crowd. His name was Zacchaeus. I bet his friends called him Zach. That is, if he had any friends. Zach was a tax collector by trade—the most despised vocation in town. The Romans had conquered the Jews and bribed Zach to turn against his own people. His job was to go door-to-door with Roman soldiers and demand that his neighbors send a percentage of their income to Caesar in Rome. But tax collectors were known for up-charging everyone, becoming rich by stealing from their own community.

SCRIPTURE

Turn in your Bible to Luke 19:1–10. Read it slowly and underline anything that catches your eye. Read the first five verses for a second time and then share your wonderings.

My Wonderings:
• I wonder how short Zach really was?

- I wonder…

- I wonder…

- I wonder…

I wonder how Jesus actually saw Zach. I just did a Google Image search of "sycamore trees" and they look like big pieces of broccoli. They have so many leaves that it would have been easy for Zach to stay hidden under cover. I wonder if Jesus was the only one who even noticed him hiding in the tree.

Maybe you feel like that sometimes. Like no one ever notices you.

You try your best to get bigger numbers on reports cards, social media posts, and in the weight room. And smaller numbers on the scale. But sometimes you mess up on purpose, just to get someone's attention.

Many of my teenage friends are asking the question "DOES ANYONE SEE ME?"

STORY

Below are some actual statements my friends have posted on their social media accounts:

- I'm screaming at the top of my lungs, and no one even turns their head.

- I hate when my mom talks about how awesome my brother and sister are. #IFeelLikeCrapNow

- Try walking a mile in my shoes, then you can yell at me for not being perfect.

- OK, I'm bored. What should I pierce?

- I wish I believed I was worth loving.

- I wasted my childhood trying to grow up.

- Leave it to me to always mess everything up.

- I told my mom I'm depressed and can't do my homework cause I'm emotionally damaged. She believed me and is taking me to the doc. LOL

- Crying because I'm so exhausted and I want to sleep but I can't because I have so much work.

- Emotionally . . . I'm done. Mentally . . . I'm drained. Spiritually . . . I feel dead. Yet physically . . . I smile.

One of my high school friends sent me this message:

Drew,

Last night . . . it hit the fan, and I mean hard. Everything was going good and then my mom had the great idea to start the timeless argument about how I don't care about school. She called me downstairs and logged into the parent portal to check my grades . . . they were bad. I had pretty much given up hope this year. As the argument continued, I found myself falling into a pit of deep-seated hatred and anger for my parents. They just don't get it, I thought. I punched my wall, 'cause that's what kids do in movies and stuff, but it kinda hurt, and I didn't feel any better. My dad is so angry. He took away all my stuff. My phone, my laptop, my friends, my driving privileges for, as he said, "the entire summer." He even told my mom to take away all my clothes except for two pairs of shorts, two pairs of shirts, two pairs of socks, and one pair of shoes. He said my life is going to be like the military. We are talking waking up early, doing chores, and yard work every day this summer. This is the worst ever. Now I know why people become alcoholics. <u>My parents just don't get what I'm going through. They don't understand my emotions. I feel like nobody understands me.</u> I have lost touch with God. I'm stupid, worthless, scrawny, ugly, too skinny, no girlfriend, and living for no reason. My parents came in to say good night to me and told me they were sorry, but they did it 'cause they love me. When they said "Goodnight, love you," all I could mumble was, "I wish the feeling was mutual."

– Ben

Do you ever feel like that? Like no one truly gets you, like no one understands you, like no one sees you?

JESUS

Jesus sees you. Just like he saw Zach hiding in that tree.

But how would you know if Jesus was looking at you right now? You would have to look at him in order to really know, right? Your eyes would need to meet his. So how do we do that? How do we turn our eyes towards Jesus?

The Message translation of Luke 19:3–4 says, "**[Zach] wanted desperately to see Jesus**, but the crowd was in his way . . . so he ran on ahead and climbed up in a sycamore tree so he could see Jesus."

Maybe we do the same thing Zach did. If we desperately want to see Jesus, maybe we figure out how to escape the chaos of the crowd and climb up a tree.

How is "the crowd" distracting you? Could it be the notifications constantly buzzing in your pocket? Is it a constant fear of missing out? What if the distractions are keeping us from missing out on the one thing we want to see most? Jesus. Can anything compare to looking into the eyes of God and seeing that he is looking back at us?

TODAY'S ALONGSIDE PRACTICE

At the heart of worship is attention. Make a list of things that are distracting you from paying attention to Jesus. Take your time and ask Jesus to reveal to you the things that are keeping you from seeing him. Then, as an act of surrender, write them down.

-
-
-
-
-

Pray something like, "Jesus, just like Zacchaeus, I desperately want to see you, but I'm distracted. Will you help me turn *from* my distractions and *toward* you?"

SONG

"Communion" by Maverick City Music

THE WEEKEND CONVERSATION

Below is a set of questions for you to talk through with your Alongsider. You'll be tempted to skip it and just move on to the next day. Fight that temptation. Call your devo-partner, or better yet, take a weekend walk together. Spend time reflecting on the past week. My guess is that it will end up being your favorite part of this whole devotional.

If you don't have an Alongsider yet, pray and ask the Lord to bring someone to mind that could walk this journey with you. If God reveals a potential partner, ask him for the courage to contact them. And then do it. You could also go over these questions with a small group or Bible study.

In the meantime, go ahead and process the questions below on your own. The best way to reflect is by writing down your answers. As you're writing them, imagine that Jesus is your Alongsider today. He is actually closer to you than anyone else ever could ever be.

1. Which day stuck out to you the most and why?
    - ❒ Jesus Shows
    - ❒ Jesus Asks
    - ❒ Jesus Listens
    - ❒ Jesus Sees

2. Which gospel story most resonates with your own life?

3. Share a few of your wonderings.

4. Which of the Alongside Practices did you enjoy most? Which helped you connect with Jesus?

➁ Turning "God is nowhere" into "God is now here"

➁ Answering Jesus's *"Do you want to get well?"* question and sharing your own need for healing

➁ Hearing someone else's story

➁ Sharing your M&M's with someone

➁ Making a list of your distractions

5. Which song did you most resonate with?

➁ "More Like Love" by Ben Rector

➁ "SOS" by We the Kingdom

➁ "I Am Your Beloved" by Jonathan David and Melissa Helser

➁ "Communion" by Maverick City Music

6. How are you understanding Jesus differently now?

7. How has your heart changed over the past week?

8. How can I can be praying for you?

WEEK 2

DAY 1: JESUS MOVES

"The Son of Man came eating and drinking, and you say, 'Here is a glutton and a drunkard, a friend of tax collectors and sinners.'"
(Luke 7:34)

QUESTION

You can learn a lot about a person by who they hang out with. Have you ever made assumptions about others, simply based on their associations?

"Oh, she's friends with her? I know what she must be like."

"He's on that team? I bet he's just like those other guys."

When we read the gospel accounts written about Jesus in the books of Matthew, Mark, Luke, and John, we get a pretty clear picture of who he spent his time with. His days were full of meals and interactions with thieves (like Zacchaeus), prostitutes, outcasts, lepers, criminals, rowdy fisherman, and the general scum of society.

A few times in the Gospels it's even recorded that people insulted Jesus by calling him a "friend of sinners."

If drones had been invented 2,000 years ago, and you watched the recording of all of Jesus's movements, you might have wondered if he was mischievous.

Maybe when you picture God, you imagine him running away from sin. I know my typical knee-jerk reaction after I mess up is to avoid God altogether. I don't want to pray, go to church, or do anything that reminds me of my sin. I'm sure God is even more disappointed in me than I am in myself. Surely, he doesn't want to be near me.

But it seems like just the opposite is true. Jesus, God with skin on, moves toward people who sin.

Look at how the psalmist describes God here:

"The Lord is close to the brokenhearted and saves those who are crushed in spirit" (Psalm 34:18).

"If your heart is broken, you'll find God right there; if you're kicked in the gut, he'll help you catch your breath" (Psalm 34:18 MSG).

Who is Jesus drawn to? Who does he move toward?

Sinners like Zacchaeus. Outcasts like me and you.

God's desire to be in relationship with us is not dependent on how good we are. It doesn't hinge on how much we sin. From reading the accounts of Jesus's life, it seems it's "not our loveliness that wins his love, but our unloveliness."[3]

SCRIPTURE

If there was a single type of person in Jesus's day who was considered the most unlovely, it was a leper. Leprosy is a disease that attacks the nerve endings and removes one's ability to feel. Lepers would often lose their fingers and toes and be covered in sores. They often reeked of a violent stench. Their smell could make you gag. The sight of them might even scare children. No one wanted to be anywhere near a leper. They were treated like monsters. Governments even established laws that required anyone with the disease to live in quarantine outside of the city. Leprosy was the ultimate mark of shame and seclusion.

And to make it worse, most people believed the sickness was a consequence of sin. If you had leprosy, you must have really made God angry. And because of that, lepers weren't just kept out of the city, they also were banned from church and not allowed to enter the temple or the synagogue. They were considered both physically and spiritually unclean.

Three different gospel writers record stories of Jesus interacting with people who had this awful disease. If you want to read them all, you can turn to: Matthew 8:1–4 or Luke 5:12–16, but today we're going to look at Mark's account in Mark 1:40–45. Go ahead and read it in your Bible.

My Wonderings:
- I wonder if the leper had any friends.

- I wonder…

- I wonder…

- I wonder…

STORY

Now, imagine the scene. Jesus is preaching in the center of town. Like usual, the crowds are pressing in around him. With their eyes focusing on the teacher, they don't see the outcast creeping into their midst. Then someone notices and starts screaming.

"What is the leper doing here? He's not allowed to be in the city! Don't touch me!"

The people peel back. A path clears for the leper to approach the healer. He stumbles before Jesus and falls on his knees. With his eyes towards the ground, the outcast whispers a prayer: "If you are willing, you can make me clean."

Mark records Christ's response this way: "**Deeply moved**, Jesus put out his hand, touched him, and said, 'I want to. Be clean'" (Mark 1:41 MSG).

In unison, the crowd gasps. "Did you see that? The teacher just touched the leper. Now Jesus is also unclean! Why would he do that?"

JESUS

Mark tells us exactly why: Jesus was moved with compassion. The Greek word used in the original language of Mark is *sphlochna*. There's not an exact translation in the English language, but the term is used to describe someone's internal organs, intestines, and bowels. What Mark is saying is that when Jesus saw the man, he literally felt like he'd been punched in the gut. His heart broke open. And when it did, love and compassion spilled out.

And then Jesus did the unthinkable.

When everyone else backed away, Jesus moved toward the man.

You can read the rest of the story and hear more about the healing and what happened next, but for now, just take a deep breath and put yourself in the leper's worn-out-shoes.

When have you felt like an outcast? From your friends, your family, from God?

No matter what you have done. No matter what has been done to you.

No matter how much you've messed up. No matter how unlovely or unlovable you feel.

Jesus moves toward you. He can't help himself. It's just who he is.

Today's Alongside Practice

Second to Jesus, there's one person whose story takes up more pages in the Bible than any other: King David. The teenage sling-shotter who first got famous by dropping Goliath in the first round. If you want to read his whole story, it's fascinating and can be found in the Old Testament between 1 Samuel 15 and 1 Kings 2.

But as many glorifying stories as there are about King David, there are also some horrifying ones. David made some massive mistakes. He was an adulterer, a murderer, and a liar. And yet, God called him "a man after my own heart" (1 Samuel 13:14; Acts 13:22).

After one of his bigger failures, David responded, not by running away from God, but by running toward him. He prayed a prayer that is found in Psalm 51. Sometimes it's hard to know how to pray. At those moments, the Psalms come in handy. They're the prayer book of the Bible. They give us words when we can't find our own.

Praying this prayer will help you believe that God actually moves towards you in your brokenness.

Go ahead and flip to **Psalm 51**. It's almost exactly in the middle of your Bible.

Read it as a prayer of confession to God. Underline words of phrases that catch your eye.

As you pray it, imagine Jesus holding you in his arms, much like how I imagine he embraced the leper.

After you read it in your translation, pray it aloud using the words from The Message paraphrase below:

Generous in love—God, give grace!
> Huge in mercy—wipe out my bad record.
Scrub away my guilt,
> soak out my sins in your laundry.
I know how bad I've been;
> my sins are staring me down.
You're the One I've violated, and you've seen
> it all, seen the full extent of my evil.
You have all the facts before you;
> whatever you decide about me is fair.
I've been out of step with you for a long time,
> in the wrong since before I was born.
What you're after is truth from the inside out.
> Enter me, then; conceive a new, true life.
Soak me in your laundry and I'll come out clean,
> scrub me and I'll have a snow-white life.
Tune me in to foot-tapping songs,
> set these once-broken bones to dancing.
Don't look too close for blemishes,
> give me a clean bill of health.
God, make a fresh start in me,
> shape a Genesis week from the chaos of my life.
Don't throw me out with the trash,
> or fail to breathe holiness in me.
Bring me back from gray exile,
> put a fresh wind in my sails!
Give me a job teaching rebels your ways
> so the lost can find their way home.
Commute my death sentence, God, my salvation God,
> and I'll sing anthems to your life-giving ways.
Unbutton my lips, dear God;
> I'll let loose with your praise.

Going through the motions doesn't please you,
    a flawless performance is nothing to you.
I learned God-worship
    when my pride was shattered.
Heart-shattered lives ready for love
    don't for a moment escape God's notice.
Make Zion the place you delight in,
    repair Jerusalem's broken-down walls.
Then you'll get real worship from us,
    acts of worship small and large,
Including all the bulls
    they can heave onto your altar!

This week, when you mess up, when you feel unlovely and unlovable, remember that Jesus doesn't turn his face away from you; he moves towards you.

*If you want to see a powerful portrayal of the scene where Jesus heals the leper, search YouTube for a four-minute clip from the TV series, "The Chosen." Search: "The Chosen Jesus heals the leper."

SONG

"Runaway" by Jess Ray

DAY 2: JESUS RESTS

"'Are you tired? Worn out? Burned out on religion? Come to me. Get away with me and you'll recover your life. I'll show you how to take a real rest. Walk with me and work with me—watch how I do it. Learn the unforced rhythms of grace. I won't lay anything heavy or ill-fitting on you. Keep company with me and you'll learn to live freely and lightly'" (Matthew 11:28–30 MSG).

QUESTION

Jesus asks, "Are you worn out? Could you use a real rest?"

Jesus wants that for you. How do find real rest?

SCRIPTURE

Open your Bible to Matthew 11:28–30 and read what your translation says. Underline it. Imagine Jesus saying those words to you right now.

Jesus says, "Take my yoke upon you and learn from me" (v. 29a).

"Walk with me and work with me—watch how I do it" (v. 29 MSG).

So, let's do what he says. Let's look at the Gospels and watch how Jesus pursues rest.

When you look at the miracles of Jesus, a clear pattern develops. It happens with almost every one of them, but let's revisit the one we looked at yesterday, the healing of the leper.

Turn to Mark 1:40. That afternoon, Jesus was healing a leper. But what was he doing that morning? Back up five verses and look at Mark 1:35 to find out.

As you think about Jesus spending time alone with the Father, what comes to mind?

My Wonderings:

- I wonder what time Jesus usually went to bed at night.

- I wonder…

- I wonder…

- I wonder…

"Very early in the morning, while it was still dark, Jesus got up, left the house and went off to a solitary place, where he prayed" (Mark 1:35).

- Hours before he healed the leper, what did Jesus do? Got up early, went off by himself, and prayed.

- Before he performed his first miracle ever, Jesus spent more than a month in the woods with his Father. (v. 12)

- Before he called his disciples to follow him, Jesus took a walk alone on the beach. (v. 16)

- Before he began casting demons out of a boy, he was fasting and praying. (Mark 9:2)

- Before he walked on water, Jesus climbed up a mountain to pray. (John 6:15)

- He spent entire nights in prayer. (Luke 6:12)

- Even the night before he was going to be crucified, Jesus was on his knees in the garden talking to his Father. (Luke 22:41)

"Jesus often withdrew to lonely places and prayed." (Luke 5:16)

Jesus says that the path to real rest is keeping company with him. That's how we learn to live in freedom. Being with Jesus is the way to experience true rest. Jesus himself is our rest.

But just like we saw last week, there are many things distracting us from "getting away to a solitary place with him."

How have the last few days been for you? Have you noticed those distractions having more or less power over you? Would you like for them to have less? If so, Jesus offers a solution in Matthew 6:16. It's found right in the middle of his most famous teaching, the Sermon on the Mount.

He makes this statement: "'When you fast . . .'" Not *if* you fast, but *when*. Jesus assumes his followers will practice the discipline of fasting. Fasting is simply voluntarily going without something. It's most commonly associated with food, but it can be done with all kinds of things, as you'll see in today's Alongside Practice.

Fasting seems strange. We live in a culture that constantly tells us we need MORE of everything, not less. More money, more entertainment, more followers, more gadgets, more clothes, and more food.

STORY

In 1955, when McDonald's opened, the original size of the fountain soda cup was 7 oz. Now you can get one SIX TIMES larger! And if 42 oz. isn't enough for you, you can get a 128 oz. Big Gulp at any 7-Eleven.[4]

Since iPhones first came out in 2007, I've personally owned at least ten different models, each one newer, faster, and better than the one I had before. We live in a world that makes us think we need MORE. Fasting takes us in the opposite direction.

There's a good chance that you've never intentionally fasted before. Maybe that's because you didn't know about it or understand why anyone would *want* to do it. Fasting is hard. The world, our flesh, and the devil often work together to keep us from it.

JESUS

What's important about fasting is to remember why we're doing it. What we long for is true rest and intimacy with God. We long for rest from worry, from striving, from pretending to be someone we're not. True rest comes from a closeness with Jesus—from a resting in who we are in him.

Lots of things get in the way of that. Fasting is a practical way to say, "No. I'm not going to pay attention to any of these distractions. I want to fix my eyes on Jesus alone."

Now when you fast, you might feel tempted to tell everyone you know about it. We somehow think others will think better of us if they know we're fasting. But listen to what Jesus says about that.

> When you practice some appetite-denying discipline to better concentrate on God, don't make a production out of it. It might turn you into a small-time celebrity but it won't make you a saint. If you 'go into training' inwardly, act normal outwardly. Shampoo and comb your hair, brush your teeth, wash your face. God doesn't require attention-getting devices. He won't overlook what you are doing; he'll reward you well. (Matthew 6:16–18 MSG)

What reward is Jesus talking about? He's talking about himself. Jesus is the reward. When we deny the other temptations vying for our attention, and spend time with him, we get to experience the true rest of knowing Jesus.

TODAY'S ALONGSIDE PRACTICE

In order to help you rest in Jesus this week, select one of the fasting options below. You might to be tempted to do more than one. Don't. Start small. You can pick another one next week if you want, but just commit to doing one for the rest of this week.

Scripture before Screen

Before you look at any screen in the morning, spend time reading God's Word. If you're looking for a place to start, turn to Matthew chapters 5–7 and read the rest of the Sermon on the Mount.

Less Time in Front of the Mirror

If you struggle with finding your identity in your appearance, or what you wear, consider spending less time in front of the mirror.

I had a friend who looked like a model. He exercised a lot and worked hard to impress others with his appearance. One day he became convicted about it. More than gaining the approval of others, he wanted to know God more deeply. To help him move towards that, he decided to spend less time focused on his appearance—less time in front of the mirror. He told me that it was crazy to see how differently people treated him when he didn't look as put together as he had before. He said that their reactions led him into a deeper rest in the steady, constant love of God.

Giving Up a Comfort

We are people who consistently run to find pleasure in anything other than God. Consider giving up something that "soothes" you for the rest of this week. A comfort food like desserts, hitting the snooze button, watching a show before bed, etc. Where do you turn for pleasure?

Limited Media

Estimate how much time you spend each week on screens. You can probably look at the "Screen Time" report in your phone settings and get an accurate estimate. Add up social media, streaming video, video games, etc. Once you get that total for the week, divide it by seven and see what your average screen time is in a single day. Once you've got that number, consider cutting it in half each day for the rest of the week. For example, if you regularly watch an average of four hours/day of Netflix and YouTube, you would limit yourself to two hours/day. If you spend two hours/day on social media, you would limit yourself to one hour/day.

You could also fast from screens for an entire day or don't look at any screens until school gets out in the afternoon. A few years ago, I fasted from screens for seven weeks. It was the most life-changing thing I've ever done. I'm convinced that fasting from screens helped re-wire my brain. My relationship with technology has been much healthier ever since.

If you're anything like me, you might not have the self-discipline to limit your own screen time. That's why I have a screen time limit set on my phone for my internet usage and time-wasting apps. After I reach my time limit each day, my phone locks me out and I don't know the password to get around it. Only my wife does. Consider asking your Alongsider to put a code in your phone to help you set some boundaries when it comes to screen time.

Words/People

If you're an extrovert, silence and solitude are probably pretty difficult practices for you to engage in. Consider giving up words or interaction with other people for part of a day. Leave your phone at home and take a walk with God.

*Remember, only pick one. And don't tell a lot of people what you're doing. Maybe just tell your parents and your Alongsider. The goal isn't to perform or be a better person. The goal is to give up something that might distract you from Jesus, in order to allow your mind and heart to find true rest in him alone.

SONG

"Turn Your Eyes Upon Jesus" by Josh Garrels

DAY 3: JESUS PRAYS

"'Here's what I want you to do: Find a quiet, secluded place so you won't be tempted to role-play before God. Just be there as simply and honestly as you can manage. The focus will shift from you to God, and you will begin to sense his grace" (Matthew 6:6 MSG).

Scripture

If there was anyone who didn't need to pray, wouldn't you think it would be the Son of God? But over and over again in the Gospels, we find Jesus on his knees, talking to his dad.

The entire chapter of John 17 is a journal of Jesus's prayers. How incredible that we get to read the very words Jesus speaks to God! If you have time now, read the whole chapter. If not, come back and read it tonight or tomorrow. As you read, pay attention to *how* Jesus prayed. Even though he was a grown man, his prayer is spoken with the voice of a child. He tells his dad the desires of his heart and prays expectantly, believing his Father is listening.

It's the very same posture when he teaches the disciples how to pray in Matthew 6. He could have taught them to begin their prayers with words like *Almighty Maker of the universe*, but instead he begins with one word: *Father*. (See Luke 11:1–4.)

These words disarm us. They signal our dependence as children. They remind us that prayer isn't a performance or a magic formula—it's a personal interaction with a living God.

Scripture

Open your Bible to Matthew 6:5–13. Jesus is preaching the Sermon on the Mount. His prayer is often referred to as the Lord's Prayer, or the "Our Father". As you read it in your

Bible, highlight the words that stick out to you, and put question marks by anything that confuses you.

For comparison, consider reading the JB Phillips translation at biblegateway.com.

Do you notice any particular pattern in the Lord's Prayer? What can we learn about Jesus's relationship with the Father?

STORY

I'll never forget my week at summer camp in the Rocky Mountains. One night, the speaker dismissed us in silence and instructed us to go sit by ourselves for twenty-minutes under the Colorado stars. I wandered to the edge of the property, leaned against a massive boulder, and assumed I would spend the next few minutes alone with God. Before I knew it, I heard someone else's feet shuffling in the dirt. I couldn't see the person, but they leaned against the other side of boulder and began to pray, unaware that I was in earshot. I don't think I'd ever heard anyone pray like that before. The voice of a teenage boy cracked as he cried out to God, overwhelmed by the undeserved love he was experiencing. The words he spoke were more honest than anything I'd ever uttered to my Heavenly Father. And though he likely never realized it, that night he taught me how to pray.

Here, in the Lord's Prayer, Jesus teaches us how to pray:

JESUS

Our Father in heaven,

Jesus begins by teaching us that our primary relationship to God is as his children.

If you aren't sure how to begin your prayers, use the word *Father*, or *Dad*, or the Hebrew word *Abba*.

Hallowed be your name, your kingdom come, your will be done, on earth as it is in heaven.

Hallowed means holy or honored. In addition to the tenderness of a Father, Jesus is teaching us to also approach God with the reverence and awe of a King. One way to practically do this is to actually get on your knees while you pray. Posture yourself in a position of submission, acknowledging to God that he is Lord and you are not.

Give us today our daily bread.

We remember that he is not only our Father and our King, but also our Provider. Everything we need and everything we have is a gift from his hands. This is a prayer of dependence.

And forgive us our debts, as we also have forgiven our debtors.

Debts is just another word for sins. God is Father, King, and Provider, but he is also a righteous judge. He asks us to confess our sin to him, and just as we receive his forgiveness, he invites us to extend that same forgiveness to others. What do you need to confess to God? Who do you need to forgive?

And do not lead us not into temptation, but deliver us from the evil one.

Life is full of temptations, but God offers to protect us and provide a way out. 1 Corinthians 10:13 says, "No temptation has overtaken you except what is common to mankind. And God is faithful; he will not let you be tempted beyond what you can bear. But when you are tempted, he will also provide a way out so that you can endure it." I once heard a pastor say that his most often prayed prayer is "God, show me danger before it comes around the corner."

For yours is the kingdom and the power and the glory forever. Amen (Matthew 6:9–13).

This part of the prayer is known as a *doxology*. It's just a way to close your prayer by telling God that he is King of all and that you worship him.

TODAY'S ALONGSIDE PRACTICE

Spending time alone with God isn't normal for most teenagers. Many of your peers aren't "wasting" their time talking to someone they can't see and praying prayers that are hundreds of years old. People your age tend to be far more concerned with the "outer-life" than the "inner-life."

When we spend time on the outer-life—what others see—it gives us immediate gratification. Getting a haircut, a new outfit, an accomplishment on the athletic field, "likes" on a social media post—those are all things that are seen by others. Prayer is different, it usually happens in secret, without anyone else knowing. But the Lord works in those quiet moments. In Scripture, God seems far more concerned with what's happening inside of us, than what everyone thinks about us.

In 1 Samuel 16:7, the Lord said to Samuel, "'Do not look on his appearance or on the height of his stature, because I have rejected him. For the Lord sees not as man sees: man looks on the outward appearance, but the Lord looks on the heart'" (ESV).

He didn't create you to be exhausted or stressed out or constantly needing the approval of others to know you're valuable. As we fix our eyes off of ourselves, and onto Jesus, we begin to see our true value and identity as children of the living God.

Remember, prayer is a conversation. It's not just a task to be completed or an item to check off of your to-do list. This is an opportunity to speak to the LORD and to listen to him. It's an opportunity to remember who he is: our Father, King,

Rescuer, and Deliverer. It's an opportunity to turn our eyes from ourselves and to behold his glory.

To practice praying like Jesus, write a translation of the Lord's Prayer below. But this time, use your own words:

SONG

"Your Love is Strong" by Jon Foreman

DAY 4: JESUS WALKS

"In the middle of their talk and questions, Jesus came up and walked
along with them . . ." (Luke 24:16 MSG).

STORY

One summer in college, I spent a month working at a camp
in the mountains of Georgia. My job was to lead a group
of high school guys who were volunteering on the outdoor
crew, which we affectionately called the ODC. Whenever we
were doing yard work around camp, I remember curiously
watching our camp director. He was always walking around
the property, slowly, with another person from the camp staff
right by his side.

On the first Wednesday of my first week, he invited
me to set down my Weed Eater™ and join him for a stroll.
We walked together for nearly an hour. I remember feeling
grateful that the head honcho wanted to spend time with me.
And that he wasn't distracted or in a hurry.

Since then, I've had the privilege of taking quite a few
walks with my friends who are your age. Walking feels quite
different from typical hangout scenarios. No eating. No
screens. No distractions. Just two friends walking together.
Sometimes in a neighborhood. Sometimes wearing a back-
pack in the woods.

One day I was eating lunch with my friend Fred, a
seasoned psychologist. We met because I wanted to ask his
advice in regard to one of my teenage friends who seemed to
be stuck in paralyzing anxiety. The first thing out of Fred's
mouth was, "You two should take walks together." He began
to tell me about something called *bilateral stimulation*. He
said that walking is actually a medically-proven therapy for
anxiety because of how it stimulates the brain.

My conversation with Fred reminded me of the year I worked at the Dale House Project in Colorado Springs. It's a halfway house for teenagers who've gone to jail, gotten released, but are not allowed to return home. Living in close quarters with twenty plus guys and gals was a recipe for short fuses to ignite. The counselor on our staff team encouraged us to handle most of the outbursts in the same way—by immediately taking a walk around the block with whoever was upset. There are few places I've encountered God's presence like I did while stomping down Cascade Avenue, alongside a steaming seventeen-year-old.

When I think back over my life, I'm surprised by how many meaningful conversations have happened over walks. The first time I told my wife, Natalie, that I loved her, we were on a walk. Every summer vacation, I take each of our kids on an unhurried, one-on-one afternoon walk down to the pier. It's one of our favorite moments of the entire year! Every Thanksgiving, my side of the family has a tradition of taking a neighborhood walk together. Even after knee-replacement surgery, my mama didn't miss it.

And remember that walk I told you about on Day One? The one I took around the lake at summer camp? There was one thing I didn't mention earlier that happened during that walk. That was the moment when I sensed Jesus inviting me into a lifetime of youth ministry. I was barely a teenager, and until then, was planning to become a professional basketball player, or at least a sports broadcaster. But that morning, on a walk, I felt Jesus nudging me to spend the rest of my life walking alongside people your age. It's been one of the greatest joys I've ever known.

QUESTION

Guess who else loves taking walks?

Scholars estimate that Jesus walked more than fifteen thousand miles in his lifetime! As you read the Gospels, notice how often Jesus is walking by a lake or through a town, sometimes by himself, sometimes with friends.

And do you know what was the first thing Jesus did after rising from the dead? He took a walk.

> Later that same day, two of Jesus' disciples were walking from Jerusalem to Emmaus, a journey of about seventeen miles. They were in the midst of a discussion about all the events of the last few days when Jesus walked up and accompanied them in their journey. They were unaware that it was actually Jesus walking alongside them. . . . (Luke 24:13–16a TPT)

Now fast-forward sixteen verses to that night when they were eating dinner together.

> Stunned, they looked at each other and said, 'Why didn't we recognize him? Didn't our hearts burn with the flames of holy passion while we walked beside him? (v. 32 TPT)

JESUS

Even though I've been walking with Jesus for years, there are many days when I forget he's with me. Even though I can't see him, I know he's real. It seems that a lot of the most important things in my life are invisible: the air I breathe, the love I feel, the hope I cling to, and the person who walks alongside me every day. Yet much like the two disciples on the road to Emmaus, I often don't recognize that Jesus is present with me.

SCRIPTURE

Open your Bibles to Luke 24. Today is going to be a longer reading than usual, but you're going to love the closing chapter. It's fifty-two verses, so grab your pen, open your imagination, and try and picture yourself as one of Jesus's disciples. What do you feel? What do you notice? What questions do you have? After you read the entire chapter, write your thoughts below.

My Wonderings:

- I wonder what it would have felt like to be one of the disciples watching the resurrected son of God eat a piece of broiled fish.

- I wonder...

- I wonder...

- I wonder...

TODAY'S ALONGSIDE PRACTICE

If my psychologist friend, Fred, is right—and walking is actually medically proven to relieve anxiety—then today's practice will be especially helpful if there's anything worrying you right now.

Your assignment is to take a thirty-minute walk by yourself sometime in the next couple of days. Make sure to leave your phone and headphones behind. Don't worry about hitting the thirty-minute mark exactly. Don't take a watch. Don't take anything that might distract you.

And don't walk for exercise. If you're sweating, you're probably walking too fast—unless you're doing this during the heat of the summer! Intentionally walk slower than normal. Like half as fast as you would normally walk.

In order to practice your pacing, I want you to write the word *slow* in the space below.

Now, I want you to write the word *slow* again, and try and take a full minute to write it. That's fifteen seconds per letter.

That was tough, wasn't it? Our natural tendency is to get stuff done and to do it as fast as possible. But when we're in a hurry, there's a lot we miss. As you go for your walk, pay attention to your breathing and to your heartbeat. Be in awe of how amazing it is that you are a living being. Pay attention to the creation around you. Notice the birds, the trees, and the sky. In order to avoid distractions, like cars and other people, I encourage you to go super early in the morning, just as the sun rises. If you're not a morning person, consider setting an alarm for tomorrow morning, and maybe even going back to bed after your walk.

If you don't live in an ideal area for taking walks, plan a time to go to a park or a trail with a friend, parent, or your Alongsider. Go there together, but plan to walk alone.

The point of this exercise is to practice slowing down and paying attention. To imagine yourself actually taking a walk with Jesus. One advantage to walking at sunrise is that you can actually pray aloud to Jesus and no one will likely hear you. I know it feels strange to talk to someone you can't see, but it actually helps us learn how to communicate with God.

It's kind of like going on a first date. On November 6, 2002, Natalie and I had our first date over dessert at an Applebee's in Salisbury, NC. It was awkward at best. We stumbled through conversation. I had no clue what I was doing. Somehow, I convinced her to join me for a second date. To try and make it less awkward, I planned for us to do an activity together, so we went hiking at Pilot Mountain. It's amazing how much easier it is to have a conversation when you're walking beside someone, and not just watching them slurp a milkshake. Now we've been married for almost twenty years and conversation is a lot more natural than it was on that first date. We take a lot of walks together. Sometimes, we talk non-stop; other times, we're silent.

That's how it'll happen with you and Jesus. It'll feel clunky at first. You'll take a morning walk and try talking to him out loud. Then a biker will pass by you and you'll get embarrassed that they overheard you talking to "no one." You'll take a walk and not know what to talk with him about. That's OK. Listening is a really important part of prayer as well. Keep showing up and the same thing will happen to you that happened to the disciples in Luke 24:31a.

"Then their eyes were opened and they recognized him . . ."

A Walking Prayer (based on Isaiah 40)

Jesus, I want to walk with you as you walked with your Father. I want to know the intimacy of true companionship with you. Teach me to walk in your ways—and as I do—to find true rest. When I walk away from you, make my footsteps heavy so I am unable to run. Teach me to walk alongside you; your footsteps lead to freedom.

* If you liked this practice and want to try more like it, check out the short book *Backyard Pilgrim* by Matt Canlis. It's a forty-day devotional that guides you through taking the same walk in your neighborhood forty days in a row. You can pick it up at LiveGodSpeed.org. There's also a pretty incredible

thirty-minute documentary film you can watch on that website called *Godspeed*. If you can find time, I'd encourage you to watch it with your family or your Alongsider.

SONG

"I Want Jesus To Walk with Me" by Paul Zach and Liz Vice

THE WEEKEND CONVERSATION

Below is a set of questions for you to talk through with your Alongsider this weekend.

1. Which day stuck out to you the most and why?
    - ❒ Jesus Moves
    - ❒ Jesus Rests
    - ❒ Jesus Prays
    - ❒ Jesus Walks

2. Which gospel story most resonates with your own life?
    - ❒ The healing of the leper
    - ❒ Jesus spending time with his Father
    - ❒ Jesus teaching the disciples how to pray
    - ❒ The resurrection story and the Road to Emmaus

3. Share a few of your wonderings.

4. Which of the Alongside Practices did you enjoy most? Which helped you connect with Jesus?
    - ❒ Praying Psalm 51
    - ❒ Watching the clip from *The Chosen*
    - ❒ Fasting
    - ❒ Re-writing the Lord's Prayer
    - ❒ Walking with Jesus

5. Why do you think those specific practices resonated with you?

- What are you fasting from? How's it going?

- What is typically the first thing you do when you wake up and the last thing you do before you go to bed? How do those habits impact you?

- Tell me about your walk. How did that go?

6. Which song did you most resonate with?

- ❒ "Runaway" by Jess Ray
- ❒ "Turn Your Eyes Upon Jesus" by Josh Garrels
- ❒ "Your Love is Strong" by Jon Foreman
- ❒ "I Want Jesus To Walk with Me" by Paul Zach and Liz Vice

7. How are you understanding Jesus differently now?

8. How has your heart changed over the past week?

9. How can I can be praying for you?

WEEK 3

DAY 1: JESUS UNDERSTANDS

"For we do not have a high priest who is unable to sympathize with our weaknesses, but we have one who has been tempted in every way, just as we are—yet without sin. Let us then approach God's throne of grace with confidence, so that we may receive mercy and find grace to help us in our time of need." (Hebrews 4:15–16)

Story

My friend Jim Branch told me a story that happened a few years ago in a high school cafeteria. He was there with a few college students and adults who were Young Life leaders at the school. Jim tells it this way:

> I overheard a commotion a few tables away and looked up to see one of the kids who came regularly to our Young Life club on Thursday nights. She had accidentally dumped her entire tray of food onto her lap. I don't remember what they were having for lunch that day, but I do remember that it was a total mess. A tray full of food was all over her pants and she was on the verge of tears. Immediately her Young Life leader, in a moment of grace and wisdom, sprang into action. She grabbed her friend and whisked her off to the restroom as she said, "Quick, let's go change pants. You take mine and I'll wear yours."

That's exactly what they did. Within minutes, the ninth-grade girl emerged from the restroom looking like nothing had ever happened. Her Young Life leader came out wearing the pants completely covered with food stains.

It seems like the best way to truly understand someone—and to deeply love someone—is to walk in their shoes, to experience their hurt and chaos with them.

JESUS

Jesus is the one person who knows exactly what you're experiencing.

The writer of Hebrews speaks of Jesus this way: "For we do not have a high priest who is unable to sympathize with our weaknesses, but we have one who has been tempted in every way, just as we are—yet without sin. Let us then approach God's throne of grace with confidence, so that we may receive mercy and find grace to help us in our time of need" (Hebrews 4:15–16).

Two-thousand years ago, Jesus put on skin and dove headfirst into our mess. He can sympathize with our weaknesses. He understands everything we are going through.

If you carefully read through the Gospels, you'll discover that you and Jesus have a lot in common:

- Jesus was born as a baby and relied upon his parents to take care of him.
- Jesus had brothers and sisters.
- Jesus went through puberty.
- Jesus ate, slept, and used the bathroom.
- Jesus spent decades in obscurity.
- Jesus never owned a horse, car, phone, or home.
- Jesus experienced hunger and thirst.

- Jesus battled temptation.
- Jesus grieved the death of his cousin and one of his best friends.
- Historians believe that Jesus's earthly father, Joseph, passed away when he was young.
- Jesus wept.
- Jesus never dated or married anyone.
- Jesus got angry and upset.
- Jesus was betrayed and abandoned by his closest friends.
- Jesus was falsely accused and unfairly persecuted. People lied about him.
- Jesus was abused and taken advantage of.
- Jesus was ridiculed, bullied, and mocked.
- Jesus suffered great physical pain.

QUESTION

Do you think he can relate to some of the things you're going through?

Even if you have experienced different circumstances from Jesus, he still understands. Even though he was never blind, he felt the pain of the blind beggar on the side of the road when he touched his eyes. Although he never had to find a date for prom, he understands what it feels like to be rejected.

SCRIPTURE

Hear the words the prophet Isaiah used to describe Jesus:

Who would have thought God's saving power would look like this? The servant grew up before God—a scrawny seedling, a scrubby plant in a parched field.

There was nothing attractive about him, nothing to cause us to take a second look. He was looked down on and passed over, a man who suffered, who knew pain firsthand. One look at him and people turned away. We looked down on him, thought he was scum. But the fact is, it was our pains he carried—our disfigurements, all the things wrong with us. We thought he brought it on himself, that God was punishing him for his own failures. But it was our sins that did that to him, that ripped and tore and crushed him—*our sins!* He took the punishment, and that made us whole. Through his bruises we get healed. We're all like sheep who've wandered off and gotten lost. We've all done our own thing, gone our own way. And God has piled all our sins, everything we've done wrong, on him, on him. (Isaiah 53:1–6 MSG)

Jesus gets us. He fully experienced what it's like to be human.

He's the most understanding person ever to live.

So why does this matter? Hebrews 4:16 gives us that answer.

"Let us then approach God's throne of grace with confidence, so that we may receive mercy and find grace to help us in our time of need."

Because Jesus has gone through the same trials and temptations we face, we can approach him with confidence, knowing that he understands.

When I was growing up, I attended six different schools. I was "the new kid" six different times. I had to find new friends to sit with in six different cafeterias. There were plenty of moments when I felt completely alone. But now, years later, no matter where I am—church, the pool, our kids' school, our neighborhood—do you know who I notice the most? Do you know who my heart breaks for the most? The new kids. The first-time visitors. The people who've just moved to town. My heart is drawn towards them because I know how they feel. I understand. And my understanding motivates me to show mercy.

In much the same way, Jesus understands you. And he longs to show you mercy and grace in your time of need. Run to him. Approach his throne trusting that he knows exactly how you feel. No one else can you love you like that.

Today's Alongside Practice

There are two practices today. One involves talking to your parents, the other involves writing to God.

Do both if possible.

1. Talking to Parents

As a teenager, you might struggle with feeling like your parents don't understand you. Like they don't quite remember what it's like to go through adolescence. And when your parents were kids, they didn't face a lot of the same trials and temptations that you do. They didn't have things like social media. They weren't judged by the number of "likes" on their pictures. The pressures are certainly different today.

One way you can help bridge the understanding gap between you and your parents is by moving towards them. If you want them to try to put themselves in your shoes, a great start is to put yourself in theirs.

Over dinner tonight, consider asking your parents at least one of the following questions:

- What is something hard you went through when you were my age?

- What is a challenge you're currently facing that I maybe don't fully understand?

- What are some of the hard parts of being an adult that I'm maybe not fully aware of?

2. Journaling

Have you ever written a note to God? Give it a shot and just tell him how you feel. He cares and he wants to hear from you. If you don't have a journal, you could write on one of the blank pages in the back of this book. Or get an old school notebook. Or just a piece of paper.

If journaling is something new to you, it'll probably feel difficult at first, like writing with your off-hand, but it'll get easier. Writing, rather than just praying, helps slow us down and pay attention to God. It also helps us put our feelings into words.

The night before our wedding, Natalie gave me a gift I'll cherish forever. It's this thick brown journal with a cross on the front. It's a prayer journal filled with hundreds of pages of prayers that she prayed for her future husband. She started keeping it years before we ever met. It's amazing to read through it, remembering different seasons and circumstances, noticing how God was at work.

Instead of approaching journaling as homework, enter into this time more like a young child. View it as an adventure. Treat your pen like a sailboat and set off to explore where God wants to take you. Show yourself grace. Feel free to doodle. Draw a picture. Write bubble letters. Don't stress about spelling and grammar. And don't worry about anyone else ever reading it. This is a private letter and conversation—just between you and God.

SONG

"Before the Throne of God Above" by The Worship Initiative

DAY 2: JESUS CALMS

"Jesus was in the stern, sleeping on a cushion. The disciples woke him and said to him, 'Teacher, don't you care if we drown?'" (Mark 4:38).

QUESTION

There've been plenty of moments when I've asked Jesus the exact same question: *Don't you care if I drown?*

Maybe you can relate:

- Have you ever felt like you were drowning in schoolwork and the stress felt like an anchor tied to your ankles, pulling you under?
- Have you felt pressure from your parents or coaches or teachers or friends to perform in a certain way? Or look a certain way?
- Have you been overwhelmed, worrying what other people think about you?
- Have you ever felt left out, alone, rejected and just wanted to run away from a situation?
- Have you ever experienced so much anxiety that you literally couldn't move—like you were paralyzed?

If you've ever felt any of those things, you're not alone. I know how you feel. The disciples know how you feel. And like we talked about yesterday, Jesus knows how you feel. But not only does he understand, he also provides a way out. His presence is light in darkness. His breath is peace in chaos. His voice calms any storm.

SCRIPTURE

Go ahead and turn to today's passage in Mark 4:35–41. Read how Jesus responded when the disciples experienced some of the same feelings you are. As you read, try to picture yourself in the middle of a tsunami, seasick on a boat. Use your imagination to engage the text. Then share your thoughts below.

My Wonderings:

• I wonder what kind of cushion Jesus was sleeping on?

• I wonder . . .

• I wonder . . .

• I wonder . . .

In verse 38, it's pretty clear what the disciples wondered. They wondered if Jesus even cared if they drowned. Do you wonder if God actually cares about *you*? Or is he just sleeping while your life is sinking?

STORY

When I was a teenager, I had a lot of "friends", but few that felt like real friends. Especially guys. I begged God to give me friends who wanted to follow Jesus with me, but all I heard back was silence. It felt like he couldn't hear me. Or if he could, that he was just ignoring me. It wasn't until my sophomore year of high school that a kid named Matthew moved to my hometown and showed up at my church and school. He was the answer to years of prayer. What I didn't realize at the time, was that while I was praying for a friend, I was actually developing a deeper friendship with God. Jesus was answering my prayer for a friend with himself.

JESUS

Jesus answered the disciples' question 2,000 years ago. And he answers yours the same way. How do we know he cares?

First of all, he was not taking a nap on the shore, he was in the boat *with* the disciples. He also was in the middle of the storm. If their boat went down, he was going down. **And he is in your storm with you.**

But he didn't let the boat go down, did he? With a single word, he silenced the storm. When he spoke, " . . . the wind ran out of breath. The sea became smooth as glass" (Mark 4:39–40 MSG).

And then he asked his closest friends two questions:

"Why are you so afraid? Do you still have no faith?" (Mark 4:40)

In the introduction of this book, I shared what one of the disciples wrote near the end of his gospel. After writing the whole book of John, this guy—who was actually with Jesus on the boat—explained why he wrote those twenty-one chapters.

These [stories] are written that you may believe that Jesus is the Messiah, the Son of God, and that by believing you may have life in his name. (John 20:31)

Now here's the curious thing. In the days and weeks before Jesus was snoozing in the storm, John had already watched him do plenty of miracles. Jesus had cleansed lepers, made lame people walk, cast out demons, and even made a widow's dead son come back to life. He'd witnessed all of that firsthand, and yet, in the middle of that storm, he still lacked faith. He still wondered if Jesus cared about him. He still questioned if the Son of God had enough power to stop a storm.

And over and over again, Jesus continued showing John and all of the disciples the truth about who he was. That he was God with skin on. And it seems like by the end of his book, John was finally convinced. What convinced him?

In the verses leading up to John 20:31, we see the account of Jesus appearing to his disciples after he had risen from the dead. John had watched him be nailed to the cross and witnessed Jesus breathing his final breath. John saw what every other witness saw. On a Friday night, he watched Jesus die. But on Sunday night, he saw something even more unbelievable. He encountered the risen Son of God.

It's worth checking this out for yourself. Turn and read John 20:19–22. Then reread it and write your thoughts.

My Wonderings:

- I wonder if Jesus knew how to pick locks.

- I wonder . . .

- I wonder . . .

- I wonder . . .

Did you notice what Jesus said to his disciples? He repeated it twice.

Write those four words in your book as a reminder of what Jesus is saying to you right now.

It was almost like Jesus was calming another storm. Can you imagine how fast their hearts must have been racing when they watched a dead man walk into a locked room? I bet you five bucks at least one of those guys peed his pants.

But on the evening of the resurrection, they had a slightly different reaction than they did the night of the storm.

During the storm, after Jesus exhaled peace and the wind ran out of breath, Mark records that the disciples "**were terrified and asked each other, 'Who is this? Even the wind and the waves obey him!'**" (Mark 4:41).

At that point, they were still trying to figure out who Jesus was.

But by Sunday night, they had learned the answer to their previous question.

In John 20:19, they were still terrified disciples. They hid behind a locked door for fear that the Romans would kill them like they had killed Jesus. But in a single moment—one they would never forget—their fear vanished. Jesus's presence turned their worry into worship.

John records it this way: "**The disciples were overjoyed when they saw the Lord**" (John 20:20b).

No longer were they asking "Who is this?"

With joy, they were declaring "This is the Lord!"

There will be moments in your life when you find yourself overcome with worry, shaking in the middle of a storm. There will be days when you're so afraid, you just want to hide behind a locked door. When those moments come, repeat these things aloud:

- Jesus, you are with me.
- Jesus, your very breath has the power to calm every storm.

- Jesus, you defeated death and you want to destroy anything that wants to destroy me.

- Jesus, there is no moment when you are not taking care of me.

TODAY'S ALONGSIDE PRACTICE

I wonder how long it took before the disciples finally went to wake up Jesus. Did they grab some buckets and try to bail out the water first? Did they try to paddle like a rowing team and quickly race to shore? It seems like they didn't have much faith in him at first, so why would they run to him before exhausting their own efforts?

Don't we often do the same thing? When we face anxiety and fear, we tend to just run to God as a last resort. What would it look like for you to run to him first?

For today's practice, I want to invite you to do a little exercise that might feel childish at first, but give it a shot anyway. Some people call it Imaginative Prayer.

I want you to remember a time when you've recently felt anxious.

- Maybe you were all alone at an event.

- Maybe you were being watched or evaluated by others.

- Maybe you were taking a test at school.

- Or picking out an outfit.

- Or trying to decide if you're going to sign up for summer camp.

- Maybe you felt that anxiety meter rising as you listened to your parents arguing.

- Or worrying about money.

- Or maybe, like the disciples, you had questions for God.

Try to recall how you felt in that moment. Where were you when it happened? What thoughts raced through your mind? What happened to your body? Did your heart start beating faster?

Think about what you *heard*. The disciples heard the storm and the waves. They likely heard each other panicking. If your anxious moment happened while taking a test, maybe you heard the ticking of the clock or the buzzing of the lights. If you were being watched or evaluated, maybe you heard the voice of judgment. When you walk through various storms, you will hear things—things that might seem louder than the voice and presence of Jesus. As you turn to him and cry out with your questions, listen to his response. Imagine he is with you.

After you read this next part, I want you to close your eyes and try to relive that anxious moment in your mind. **But this time, imagine that Jesus is with you.**

Picture him holding you. Lying in bed beside you. Sitting in the classroom next to you. Walking onto that playing field alongside you.

Talk to him. Tell him what you're feeling. If you're able, say it out loud.

Don't rush it. Take your time. What do you see in Jesus's eyes when he looks into yours?

What does Jesus want to say to you?

Could it be the same thing he said to the wind? **"Be still."**

Could it be the same thing he told his disciples that Sunday night? **"Peace be with you."**

Fear and worry control us as long as we think we are alone. The next time you face an anxious situation, picture Jesus there with you. He rose from the dead. He's still alive. And he lives in you.

> I have been crucified with Christ and I no longer live, but Christ lives in me. The life I now live in the body, I live by faith in the Son of God, who loved me and gave himself for me. (Galatians 2:20)

> Christ be with you. Christ within you.
> Christ behind you. Christ before you.
> Christ beside you. Christ to win you.
> Christ to comfort and restore you.
> Christ beneath you. Christ above you.
> Christ in quiet and in danger.
> Christ in hearts of those who love you.
> Christ in mouth of friend and stranger.
> Amen.
>
> -St. Patrick[5]

SONG

"Christ Be All Around Me" by All Sons & Daughters

DAY 3: JESUS CORRECTS

"While all the people were listening, Jesus said to his disciples,
'Beware of the teachers of the law. They like to walk around in flowing
robes and love to be greeted with respect in the marketplaces and
have the most important seats in the synagogues and the places of
honor at banquets. They devour widows' houses and for a show make
lengthy prayers. These men will be punished most severely'"
(Luke 20:45–47).

QUESTION

Have you ever read passages in Scripture where Jesus is cor-
recting people? He's not shaking his finger at the usual sus-
pects. He's not yelling at the liars, thieves, prostitutes, and
drunkards. His remarks are actually directed towards the
so-called religious leaders of the day.

Look at what Jesus says to them in Matthew 23:13 (MSG):

"I've had it with you! You're hopeless, you religion
scholars, you Pharisees! Frauds! Your lives are road-
blocks to God's kingdom . . ."

That's pretty harsh. Seems like Jesus detests pride. When
he sees people pretending to have it all together and acting
like they're better than everyone else, it gets on his last nerve.
It breaks his heart.

SCRIPTURE

Open your Bible to John 8:1–11. Slowly read the encounter
Jesus has with a woman who understands what it's like to be
judged. Try to imagine being in the crowd that day.

What do you notice? What do you wonder?

My Wonderings:

- I wonder . . .

- I wonder . . .

- I wonder . . .

One morning at dawn, Jesus appeared in the temple courts of Jerusalem. He was teaching a crowd of people when all of a sudden, he was interrupted. The religious leaders of the day, the Pharisees, didn't like the attention everyone was giving Jesus, so they came up with a scheme to trap him. They brought him a woman who'd been caught in adultery. I imagine they didn't give her time to get dressed. The morality police dragged her like a rag doll through the city streets, only a bed sheet covering her shame. Following their parade, they threw her at the feet of Jesus.

> "Teacher . . . in the Law Moses commanded us to stone such women. Now what do you say?" (John 8:4–5)

It was true. In the Torah (the first five books of the Hebrew Bible), the Scriptures commanded the death of adulterers. God takes the marriage covenant very seriously. The Pharisees knew Jesus, put in this situation, would have only two options. He could demand justice and order her execution. Or he could let her off the hook and go directly against the Law. They were sure they had him trapped.

JESUS
But what did Jesus do? John 8:6b records that "Jesus bent down and started to write on the ground with his finger." What on earth was he doing? Was he stumped and trying to figure out a game plan? Was he stalling? As he started to write in the sand, every accusing eye became fixated on his words. As they tried to figure out what he was writing, their attention was drawn away from the woman who'd been shaking in shame. The Scriptures tell us, "When they kept on

questioning him, he straightened up" (v.7a). I imagine Jesus standing tall, like an older sibling protecting a younger sibling. And then Jesus said those famous words: "'Let any one of you who is without sin be the first to throw a stone'" (v. 7b).

As it got quiet, the woman eventually peeked out from behind her long, tangled hair.

Jesus then stooped down to write on the ground for a second time. I wonder if this time he started writing people's names with a list of their sins. Can you imagine being a religious leader and watching Jesus write your name and sins in front of all your co-workers and neighbors? Maybe that wasn't exactly what Jesus did, but something significant happened after he asked that question. Everyone who had picked up a rock—poised to cast judgment—suddenly experienced conviction. Stones began dropping like a meteor shower. Soon the once-busy temple courts cleared out, and only Jesus and the woman remained.

Then, Jesus asked two more questions:

"'Where are they? Has no one condemned you?' 'No one, sir,' she said.

'Then neither do I condemn you,' Jesus declared. 'Go now and leave your life of sin'" (vv. 10b–11).

This didn't just happen once. Everywhere Jesus went, he treated sinners similarly. Remember Zacchaeus? Jesus didn't point up in the tree and call out his sin, "Hey, everybody, look at that traitor and thief!" He didn't wash every one of the disciples' feet except Judas's. In fact, not once in all of the Gospels did Jesus condemn a pagan. The only people he condemned were the rigid, religious people who were more concerned about their appearance of piety.

It's so opposite of the way we live. We tend to create this obscure ranking system of people who are better than others. People who are closer to God, and others who are farther away. Maybe in your mind, it looks something like this.

GOD

GOODIE-GOODIE
CUSSER
LIAR
SCHOOLWORK CHEATER
BEER DRINKER
PORN WATCHER
STEALER
DRUG USER
GIRLFRIEND/BOYFRIEND CHEATER
ABUSER
MURDERER

But that's not how Jesus treated people.

If there was any ranking system at all, maybe it would have looked like this:

JESUS

THE HUMBLE
THE PROUD

"God opposes the proud, but shows favor to the humble" (James 4:6).

If we're honest, that doesn't feel fair to us. We want to be rewarded for our good deeds, and we want others to be punished for their sins. It's easy for us to start slipping into the same trap of the Pharisees, thinking we can earn God's favor by our behavior. But as we look to Jesus, over and over again we see that the thing he most desires is for us to put our faith in his goodness—not our own. For us to confess our need for him. For us to receive his undeserved grace.

TODAY'S ALONGSIDE PRACTICE

For today's exercise, I want you to jump on YouTube and search for a clip from the 1998 version of the movie *Les Misérables*. Type the words: *Les Misérables Candlesticks Scene*. There is a newer version of the film that came out in 2012, but look for the scene with Liam Neeson. You could also use the phrase, *I give you back to God*, to narrow the search.

Before you watch the clip, here's the backstory. Victor Hugo wrote *Les Misérables* over 150 years ago and it became one of the greatest novels of the 19th century. It's the story of Jean Valjean, an ex-convict, who was finally released after nineteen years of hard labor in prison. On his first days of freedom, he wandered the streets with nowhere to go. Valjean was finally taken in by a kind old priest and his wife. During the middle of the night, in a desperate act, he steals the pastor's silver and the YouTube clip begins there. Now, go watch it and then come back.

As the bishop looked deeply in Jean Valjean's eyes, he handed him the candlesticks.

"Now don't forget it, don't you ever forget it. You've promised to become a new man."

Valjean asks the bishop, "Now why are you doing this?"

The bishop responds, "Jean Valjean, my brother, you no longer belong to evil. With this silver, I've bought your soul. I've ransomed you from fear and hatred, and now I give you back to God."

From that moment forward, Jean Valjean was never the same. He had been changed from the inside out. What changed him? Trying harder to be a better man? No. Grace changed him. Love changed him. Mercy changed him. He was given a gift he didn't deserve.

When I look at the transformations that have happened in my own life, I see a clear pattern. The times when I try to take control and make personal changes, my behavioral modifications tend to fizzle out and be short-lived. But the moments when I encounter undeserved love, those are the instances of catalytic change. Few things transform us like grace.

I wonder whatever happened to the woman caught in adultery. I can only imagine how her life was radically changed by Jesus's grace. I wonder if, a year later, she was still there in the city the day they hung Jesus on the cross. Under the law, the penalty for her offense of adultery was execution by stoning. When a Roman citizen was convicted of a crime, they were thrown into prison. A certificate of debt, listing all their crimes, was nailed to the door of their cell. Anyone who passed by could read their list of punishable offenses. After the prisoner had served their sentence, the indictment was removed from the door. Upon their release, the judge would sign the indictment, and write across it the Greek word *tetelestai,* which means, "it is completed." The prisoner would then forever carry that document as proof that their sentence had been served, their debt had been paid, and they were truly free.

On the cross, just before Jesus breathed his last, he cried out that very same word: **tetelestai. It is finished!**

My debt. Your debt. The debt of the adulterous woman. All paid in full by the perfect sacrifice of the Son of God. Jesus took that certificate of debt and completely obliterated it. He paid the very last cent of the wages of our sin. Just like the adulterous woman, we are no longer condemned. It's unbelievable, but it's true.

SONG

"His Mercy Is More" by Matt Papa

DAY 4: JESUS REDEFINES

"And they began to argue among themselves as to who would have the highest rank in the coming Kingdom. Jesus told them, 'In this world the kings and great men order their slaves around, and the slaves have no choice but to like it! But among you, the one who serves you best will be your leader. Out in the world the master sits at the table and is served by his servants. But not here! For I am your servant" (Luke 22:24–27 TLB).

QUESTION

Have you ever longed to be the greatest? Greater than your peers and their achievements, greater than last year's scores, greater than your siblings?

STORY

Confession time. During my senior year in high school, I was the editor of the school newspaper. Toward the end of the school year, we prepared to run a special edition issue focused on Senior Superlatives. Each senior got to vote for one guy and one gal in each category: Coolest Car, Class Clown, Most Outgoing, Best Hair, Most Athletic, Best Looking, Most Likely to be President, Biggest Flirt, etc. For three years, I'd read that issue of the school paper and had one single goal in mind: To be voted "Most Likely to Succeed". In my mind, being selected by my peers for that award would be the pinnacle of high school.

As the editor-in-chief, I was in the room when the votes were counted. The chalk marks on the blackboard showed that I was neck and neck with Jon Shepherd for the lead. Ashley Wall was in third place. When the chalk dust settled, Jon had beaten me by two votes. It was at that point I used my "editorial power" to change the rules. No longer would the top male and female vote-getters be selected, but I suggested it would be fairer to let the top three in every category be considered the winners. I'm not sure how I sweet-talked that teacher-sponsor into going with my new plan, but I still have a copy of that newspaper issue with my name listed right underneath Jon Shepherd's. I longed to be the greatest so much that I lied to my entire school. Most likely to succeed? More like "most likely to cheat to get what I want".

The night before Jesus was crucified, he gathered with his closest friends. Some of them remind me a lot of high school Drew. That night they were celebrating the Passover Feast. It was a meal the people of Israel celebrated every year to remember how God had rescued them from slavery in Egypt. It was kind of like Thanksgiving dinner for us, but even more significant. People now refer to it as the Last Supper.

During this meal of thanksgiving, the disciples quickly lost focus on God. Instead of enjoying the celebration and being filled with gratitude, they began to argue over which of them was the greatest. We do the same thing. When you get that test score back, you know you want to look at your class-mate's paper and see if you did better than them. We count our number of followers on social media. We brag about our video game rank. Just like the disciples, this desire to be the greatest is deep in our DNA.

SCRIPTURE

Instead of giving his followers a lecture on true greatness, Jesus did what he always does: he modeled it. Turn to John 13:1–17. Once again, imagine yourself sitting at that dinner table. Pretend you're the thirteenth disciple. Read the verses and put yourself in the story. What do you wonder?

My Wonderings:

- I wonder if any of the disciples had ever had someone else touch their feet before

- I wonder . . .

- I wonder . . .

- I wonder . . .

JESUS

How did Jesus model greatness? By washing his friends' nasty feet. The task of foot washing was so degrading that historical records document that even Jewish slaves were exempt from it. It was demeaning. Their feet were downright disgusting after walking in the sun-scorched dirt all day. But they needed to be washed. They were going to have a fancy meal together and likely didn't have chairs, so it was customary to sit on the floor—with their feet right by the food.

Imagine your sibling coming home from soccer practice. You smell the stench of their cleats and shin guards. Would you ever offer to wash their feet?

Speaking of sports, I've lived most of my athletic life content with not being the greatest. The only thing I really cared about was not getting picked last. When Jesus washed his disciples' feet, he was saying, "I'll be last. I'll be the least."

But that's the opposite message we hear from the world. I bet you're already feeling so much pressure to climb that ladder of success. To excel in sports. To win the awards. To grow in popularity. To make the grade. To build your resume. To get into the right college. To build your platform. To get the best job. To marry out of your league. To have enough money to never need to depend on anyone else. To reach that elusive American Dream. **But instead of climbing up that ladder of**

success, Jesus climbs down. He redefines greatness and says, "If you want to be great, become the least."

> [Jesus] rose from supper. He laid aside his outer garments, and taking a towel, tied it around his waist. Then he poured water into a basin and began to wash the disciples' feet and to wipe them with the towel that was wrapped around him. (John 13:4–5 ESV)

Can you picture the Son of God taking off his robe, and bare-chested, tying a towel around his waist? What is he doing? He's showing us who God is. The God who took off the robe of heaven and put on skin so that he might take on our filth and our sin.

The reality of that moment was that the disciples' feet looked a lot like their hearts. In John 13:6, Peter was next in line to have his feet washed by Jesus, but he wasn't about to have it. I'm not sure why he felt that way. Maybe Pete was embarrassed by how dirty he was. It's why I brush my teeth the hardest right before I go to the dentist. Maybe he wanted to clean himself up a little before he let Jesus see his mess.

Peter said, "'Lord, do you wash my feet?'" "'You shall never wash my feet'" (vv. 6b, 8a ESV).

But Jesus responds, "'If I do not wash you, you have no share with me'" (v. 8b ESV).

Jesus is saying, "You can't clean yourself. You can try and be a better person, but there's no way you can climb a ladder high enough to get to God. You need me to clean you. Come to me as you are, in all your filth, and I will make you clean. My love for your is not contingent on how dirty you are."

Then Jesus gives further instructions: "If I then, your Lord and Teacher, have washed your feet, you also ought to wash one another's feet. For I have given you an example, that you also should do just as I have done to you" (John 13:14–15 ESV).

But this isn't an invitation to be a better person. This is an invitation to first receive grace from Jesus and then to give that same grace away. Only when we grasp the mercy that has been shown to us, will we be able to share it with others. Like Jean Valjean—when we realize we're the ones who have both stolen the silver *and* received the candlesticks— will we be moved in service to others. That's how we become great—by becoming the least.

If we don't grasp the ugliness of our own sin and the beauty of God's grace, then serving others just becomes another way we try to manipulate our climb up the ladder to God.

So how can we test our hearts to see if we are just serving ourselves or truly serving God and others? In his classic, *The Celebration of Discipline*, Richard Foster offers a helpful explanation of false service versus true service. It is summarized below:

> *False service* (self-righteous service) comes through human effort.
> *True service* comes from a relationship with Jesus, an unselfish desire given to us by God.
>
> *False service* needs external rewards, to be noticed, appreciated, and sometimes even compensated.
> *True service* is content in being unknown and no one ever finding out.
>
> *False service* expects that the favor will be returned.
> *True service* expects nothing back, just delights in serving.
>
> *False service* is picky about who is served and discriminates based on if they can benefit me.
> *True service* serves where there is need.

False service is limited by your mood and if you "feel" like serving.
True service listens to God and is motivated by divine promptings.

False service puts others into your debt, is selfish, and uses subtle manipulation.
True service gives with no strings attached.

False service occurs when it's convenient.
True service is a regular pattern of living, it's who you are.

There's a big difference in *choosing* to do acts of service and in *being* a servant.

The first one is exhausting. The second can only happen when Christ lives in us.[6]

TODAY'S ALONGSIDE PRACTICE

Author Brennan Manning once said, "You are never more Christlike then when you are choked with compassion for the brokenness of others."[7] In the next few days, ask Jesus to fill you with so much compassion for others that you can't help but find ways to serve them. But when you serve, do it in secret. Is there something small, but significant that you could do to bless someone else?

Below are some ideas:

• Do you feel compassion for your parents and the countless ways they serve in your home? Could you help them by doing some chores that aren't already required of you? Like washing dishes, folding laundry, or mowing the grass?

• Do you feel compassion for those who might be older and less active? Imagine how encouraging it would be for one of your elderly friends or grandparents to receive a hand-written note in the mail?

- Do you feel compassion for those younger than you? Could you give up some screen time and instead play with a younger sibling, cousin or neighbor?

- Do you feel compassion for the poor and those with less than you? What if you donated clothes/money/food to the needy?

- Do you feel compassion for those in the margins? What if, instead of sitting with your normal crew, you sat with an "outsider" during school lunch and made them feel noticed and valued?

- Do you feel compassion for the homeless? Imagine if you had no bed to call your own. Could you spend one morning serving with your Alongsider at a soup kitchen?

- Do you feel compassion for the earth? What if you planted some flowers or vegetables or picked up trash on your school grounds?

- . . . and if you want to get on the real dirty footwashing level, you could even clean your siblings' or parents' bathroom!

Is there a way you could do it without drawing attention to yourself or getting praise for it?

Remember, the best way to truly become a servant is to remember how Jesus has served you. Ask him to give you his compassion for others.

SONG

"Sandcastles" by Skye Peterson

THE WEEKEND CONVERSATION

Below is a set of questions for you to talk through with your Alongsider this weekend.

1. Which day stuck out to you the most and why?

   ❏ Jesus Understands

   ❏ Jesus Calms

   ❏ Jesus Condemns

   ❏ Jesus Redefines

2. Which gospel story most resonates with your own life?

   ❏ The calming of the storm in Mark 4

   ❏ Jesus entering the locked room in John 20

   ❏ The adulterous woman in John 8

   ❏ The footwashing in John 13

3. Share a few of your wonderings.

4. Which of the Alongside Practices did you enjoy most? Which helped you connect with Jesus?

   ❏ Asking your parents questions

   ❏ Journaling

   ❏ Imaginative Prayer (picturing Jesus with you when you're anxious)

❏ Watching the clip from *Les Misérables*

❏ Secret acts of service

5. Why do you think those specific practices resonated with you?

• What was it like talking to your parents?

• Did you find it challenging or easy to journal? What did you write about? Did you draw anything?

• Have you been able to picture Jesus being with you in recent anxious moments?

• Did you feel any emotions as you watched the movie clip?

• If you want to share, I'd love to hear your secret act of service.

6. Which song did you most resonate with?

❏ "Before the Throne of God Above" by The Worship Initiative

❏ "Christ Be All Around Me" by All Sons & Daughters

❏ "His Mercy is More" by Matt Papa

❏ "Sandcastles" by Skye Peterson

7. How are you understanding Jesus differently now?

8. How was your heart changed over this past week?

9. How can I be praying for you?

WEEK 4

DAY 1: JESUS HATES

Today's devo will take you a little longer than the others. Try to carve out forty minutes if you can. If you don't have that much time, split it up in two parts. For the first part, **READ JOHN CHAPTERS 18 AND 19**. Then come back later for the devo.

> . . . for all have sinned and fall short of the glory of God. (Romans 3:23)

> . . . the wages of sin is death. (Romans 6:23a)

> This is how much God loved the world: He gave his Son, his one and only Son. And this is why: so that no one need be destroyed; by believing in him, anyone can have a whole and lasting life. God didn't go to all the trouble of sending his Son merely to point an accusing finger, telling the world how bad it was. He came to help, to put the world right again. (John 3:16–17 MSG)

STORY

Soon after we became parents, my wife Natalie and I went to see a low-budget movie on the recommendation of a friend.[8] The opening scene had us holding our breath. The main character, Nathan, pulls up to a gas station driving a top-of-the-line extended cab pickup truck. He fills up his tank and cranks the engine to leave. Right before jumping back in the truck, at the last minute, he decides to clean the bugs off his windshield. There's no water in the bucket. He grabs the squeegee and walks over to the next pump to get it wet. When he turns around, he sees a car thief hijacking his truck and screeching away. Like a madman, Nathan leaps onto his truck, barely hanging onto the steering wheel through the open driver's side window. The thief pulls on Nathan's arm, trying to pry it off the steering wheel, all while swerving and speeding down a busy road. Ultimately, Nathan is tossed to the ground just as the hijacker smashes the truck into a tree. For a moment, everything is still. The thief quickly wakes up after the crash and escapes on foot, while Nathan gradually begins to move. Traffic is stopped. Cars pull over. Bystanders call 911. Nathan attempts to crawl toward the vehicle, and a concerned woman begs, "Sir, just lie still. Don't worry about the car." Nathan pulls himself up and firmly responds, "I'm not worried about the car." He grabs the handle of the back door, and as it swings open, we see his baby boy—screaming in fear but unharmed in his car seat. Only two minutes into the movie and at the sound of his son's cries, nearly everyone watching was in tears. Now everything made sense. Seconds earlier, I was thinking, "It's just a truck; it's not worth dying over. Let it go, bro!" But seeing that little baby boy, so innocent, so scared—there was absolutely no question why Nathan risked his life. The only thing on his mind was saving his son.

I know it's just a made-up movie, but imagine if it was real, or based on a true story, or if it was actually *your* story. Wouldn't it be fun to tell your friends about that? "When I was a baby, I got kidnapped and my dad chased the guy down, wrecked his truck, and saved my life!"

Although it probably hasn't made it into a movie, your life story is more similar to that than you might realize.

Think about all the things that have tried to hijack your heart and mind: fear, anxiety, greed, stress, guilt, addictions, shame, comparison, lust, anger, deceit—the list goes on and on. Maybe you don't remember experiencing many of those things as a child, but now that you've entered your adolescent years, life feels a little more complicated. All of a sudden, you're more worried about what other people think of you. Maybe it feels like you've traded the freedom of childhood for a prison of performance.

QUESTION

Do you ever feel trapped by fear or worry or secrets? Just as Nathan chased after his infant in the car seat, God chases after you. He wants to destroy anything that wants to destroy you. God hates sin!

- If you have ever been mocked or bullied, you know why God hates sin.
- If you have ever heard your parents fighting in the room next door, you know why God hates sin.
- If you have ever been cheated on, or betrayed by a friend, you know why God hates sin.
- If you have ever given your body away and your heart went with it, you know why God hates sin.
- If you have ever been lied to, you know why God hates sin.
- If you or a loved one have ever been stuck in an addiction you can't escape, you know why God hates sin.[9]

And do you want to know how serious God is about this? It's such a big deal that it cost Jesus, the Son of God, his very life. If you want to know what a judge thinks about a crime, you look at the punishment he hands down. If you want to know what God thinks about sin, you look at the cross.

SCRIPTURE

For today's gospel reading, you're invited to spend some extended time looking at the apostle John's recording of the crucifixion. This will be your longest Scripture reading of the whole devo. Maybe you've never read these two chapters before. Take your time. Try to immerse yourself in one of the most documented events in all of history. Imagine being there. What do you see, hear, smell, feel? As you read all of John 18 and 19, record your wonders below. With such a long reading, you'll probably have more than usual.

My Wonderings:
- I wonder what the garden looked like . . .

- I wonder . . .

- I wonder . . .

- I wonder . . .

- I wonder . . .

- I wonder . . .

- I wonder . . .

- I wonder . . .

- I wonder . . .

Crucifixion was the worst kind of death possible. The Romans had mastered the art of public torture. They did it to scare people into not committing crimes. But the punishment didn't all take place while hanging on a cross. It began with flogging—a type of torment that involved tying a prisoner to a pole and then beating them with a whip. (See John 19:1.) But it wasn't just any old whip. Flogging whips were called *flagrums*, solid poles with leather cords attached. Often embedded in each strand of leather was rock, lead, glass, or bone. It severed the skin, like deep scratches from a lion's claw. The soldier who wielded the whip had one job—to bring the convict as close to death as possible without killing them. They saved the final blow for the cross.

JESUS

In Matthew's crucifixion account, he records that the soldiers spit in Jesus's face and punched him with their fists (Matthew 26:67). They mocked Jesus as "king" and smashed a crown of thorns through his hair into his skull. Then they laid his battered body on wooden beams and drove spikes through his hands and feet. Normally it took multiple soldiers to hold down a prisoner's arms, but I imagine they didn't have to wrestle Jesus. He wasn't a victim, he was a volunteer.[10] In John 10:18, Jesus said, "No one takes my life from me, but I lay it down of my own accord. I have authority to lay it down and authority to take it up again."

Why did Jesus choose to suffer in such a horrific way? To rescue us from the horrific sin that hijacks our hearts. To pay the penalty that we deserved. After Jesus had breathed his last breath, the soldiers pierced his side with a spear, and blood and water flowed out of him (John 19:34). Have you ever considered that your sin didn't just break God's rules, but it actually broke his heart?[11]

In the Old Testament, the prophet Isaiah foretold it this way, "[H]e was pierced for our transgressions, he was crushed for our iniquities; the punishment that brought us peace was on him, and by his wounds we are healed. We all, like sheep, have gone astray, each of us has turned to our own way; and the Lord has laid on him the iniquity of us all" (Isaiah 53:5–6).

When we forget how big of a deal our sin is, the cross reminds us how much it cost Jesus. God knows that sin alienates us from him and from one another and he hates it so much—because he loves us so much.

I can't imagine what I'd do if one of our children was kidnapped. I would do whatever it took to get them back. That's how Jesus feels about you. He hates sin so much that he laid down his life on the cross in order to set you free.

TODAY'S ALONGSIDE PRACTICE

Do you hate your sin? A couple of weeks ago, on the day you read about Jesus healing the leper, you prayed a prayer of confession that was written by King David in Psalm 51.

Spend some time today asking God to break your heart over your sin. Ask him to give you a hatred for sin. And then confess your sin to him.

If you're able, get on your knees and kneel before God.

Think back over your last twenty-four hours and how you have sinned against the Lord. Sometimes it helps to think about different areas of your life. Confess how you have sinned:

- In your thoughts

- In the words you've spoken

- In the acts you've committed against God and others

- In the things you ignored and neglected to do

If you need help finding words to say, below is an ancient prayer to guide you in your time of confession:

Most merciful God, I confess that I have sinned against you in thought, word, and deed, by what I have done, and by what I have left undone. I have not loved you with my whole heart; I have not loved my neighbors as myself. I am truly sorry and I humbly repent. For the sake of your Son Jesus Christ, have mercy on me and forgive me; that I may delight in your will, and walk in your ways, to the glory of your Name. Amen.[12]

SONG

"Lord Jesus, Comfort Me (A Communion Hymn)" by Matthew Smith

DAY 2: JESUS FORGIVES

"When Jesus saw their faith, he said, 'Friend, your sins are forgiven'"
(Luke 5:20).

QUESTION

Have you ever experienced moments in life when you feel like you can't move? Maybe you're exhausted. Maybe you're frozen by fear or anger. Numbed by anxiety or shame. Crippled because of things you've done or things that have been done to you, things under your control and things out of your control. Sometimes the weight can feel so heavy it's like you feel paralyzed. Two-thousand years ago, Jesus encountered a man who faced physically what you might experience emotionally.

SCRIPTURE

Read the story for yourself in Luke 5:17–26. What do you wonder?

My Wonderings:
- I wonder how the mat-carriers became friends with the paralyzed man?

- I wonder . . .

- I wonder . . .

- I wonder . . .

When I read this passage, I come away with lots of questions. I wonder how he got paralyzed in the first place? Was he born that way? Did he have an accident? Was he beaten up or abused? And how does it *feel* to have no feeling? I can't imagine a much worse state to live in. Can you imagine how desperate he must have felt? Did he even want to keep living? And who are these friends? How does he even have friends? Were they old friends who knew him before he was unable to walk?

STORY

Some years ago, I took of group of my teenage friends to a summer camp in Colorado. In the middle of the week, the camp speaker led the entire camp on a hike up Mt. Chrysolite. Three-hundred high schoolers climbing the Rocky Mountains together. The hike was no joke. The air was thin. The ground was rocky. The incline was steep. But every single camper eventually made it to the top. Even Travis.

Travis was the only kid at camp in a wheelchair. The initial plan was for him to hang back with his leader while everyone else made the summit, but once his cabinmates caught wind of the upcoming hike, they concocted a plan. The boys gathered two large timbers from the woods and borrowed a cargo net from the property staff. Once the net was secured to the timbers, they loaded it with a 250-pound linebacker and gave it a test run. It was going to take at least eight guys, four on each side, to carry Travis up that mountain. I wasn't there for the moment they surprised their buddy and told him they weren't leaving him behind. But I was there for that six-hour hike when I witnessed countless kids and leaders rotate in and help shoulder the load. I was there the moment Travis got to sit on the summit of a 13,000-foot mountain. Watching those teenage guys love their friend was even more breathtaking than the view from the top. And the smile on Travis's face seemed to stretch wider than the Colorado sky.

I wonder if that's how the paralytic felt that day in the town of Capernaum? He had likely lived so long in a state of hopelessness, but now, his buddies were carrying him on a mat to encounter the only person who could possibly heal him. I wonder if he lost hope when he saw the crowd spilling out the door. "There's no way they're going to get my stretcher inside that house." But his friends concocted a plan. They could climb the steps, remove the mud-packed tiles of the roof, tie some ropes to the mat, and lower their buddy right in front of the Healer. And everything went according to plan . . . until Jesus opened his mouth.

JESUS

> When Jesus saw their faith, he said, "Friend, your sins are forgiven." (Luke 5:20)

Can you picture the friends on the roof? Jesus smiling up at them, so pleased with their faith. And then they hear Jesus say to their crippled comrade, "Your sins are forgiven." I wonder if they about fell off the roof? I'm curious if they yelled down something like, "Excuse me, Mr. Jesus, but HE'S PARALYZED! We didn't bring him here to get his sins forgiven (umm, thanks for offering that though), but we were hoping you could make him walk again! Sorry for the confusion."

Two verses later, we see that Jesus had the ability to know what people were thinking. He could read the thoughts of both the Pharisees, who were questioning Jesus's authority to forgive sins, and the friends on the roof, who were likely questioning his ability to heal. Here's how Jesus responds:

> "Why are you thinking these things in your hearts? Which is easier: to say, 'Your sins are forgiven,' or to say, 'Get up and walk'? But I want you to know

that the Son of Man has authority on earth to forgive sins." So, he said to the paralyzed man, "I tell you, get up, take your mat and go home." (Luke 5:22b–24)

So, Jesus ends up healing the paralytic, but it's important to note the order of what Jesus did first. He addressed the internal before the external. The heart before the body. **We often come to Jesus wanting him to change our circumstances more than we desire him to forgive our sin.** We prefer him to solve our problems more than we desire him to restore our souls.

But Jesus knows that true transformation happens from the inside out. That's how he designed us. We can keep coming up with New Year's resolutions and trying to be a better person, but our efforts will always fall short. Our willpower isn't strong enough to truly change us. So, what does change us?

Forgiveness.

Yesterday, you confessed your sin to God. But why would that even matter, unless God actually has the power and the desire to forgive you? Jesus shows us that he has both.

I wonder what it was like in that jam-packed room when Jesus uttered those life-changing words. He was never in a hurry, so before he spoke, I imagine Jesus paused and knelt down beside the unmoving patient. The Son of God looked with tenderness, deep into the paralytic's eyes. Jesus rested his hands on the man's icy cheeks. And in that breathless moment, time stood still. Then, in a profound hush, Jesus spoke.

I want you to know that the Son of Man has authority on earth to forgive sins.' So, he said to the paralyzed man, "I tell you, get up, take your mat and go home. (Luke 5:24)

Then, in the sight of all, the immovable man began to move. The speechless man spoke. It began with a sobbing of deep relief. A convulsion of joy shook his entire frame. The crowd gasped as they saw an elbow move. The man's palms slowly gripped the dirt floor. He began to stand. Swaying, he gradually found his balance. Jesus held his hands. The onlookers held their breath. Certainly, there was an embrace between the Healer and the patient. The people parted, the friends rushed down from the roof, and the new man took a long stroll home.

> He did it—got up, took his blanket, and left for home, giving glory to God all the way. The people rubbed their eyes, stunned—and then also gave glory to God. Awestruck, they said, "We've never seen anything like that!" (Luke 5:25–26 MSG)

When you confess your sin to Jesus, you can rest assured that he has both the power and the desire to forgive you. You don't need to keep asking to make sure he heard. Forgiving you is what he loves to do. It's why he went to the cross. Hebrew's 12:2a puts it this way, "For the joy set before him he endured the cross." Another translation says, "For he himself endured a cross and thought nothing of its shame because of the joy he knew would follow his suffering." (PHILLIPS)

How does God forgive your sin? *To Be a Christian: An Anglican Catechism* answers it this way: "By virtue of Christ's atoning sacrifice [on the cross], God sets aside my sins, accepts me, and adopts me as his child and heir in Jesus Christ. Loving me as his child, he forgives my sins whenever I turn to him in repentance and faith."[13]

How should you respond to God's forgiveness? "Trusting in God's continual forgiveness, I should live in continual thanks, praise, and obedience to him; and as I have been loved and forgiven by God, so I should love and forgive those who sin against me" (Psalm 51:7–17; Isaiah 44:21–23; Matthew 6:12; 18:21–35; Ephesians 4:32).[14]

You are his joy. Forgiving you isn't painful to Jesus. He already endured the pain of the cross. He isn't stingy with his love. Jesus delights in giving forgiveness. The biggest problem in the world is alienation, and the cure for alienation is forgiveness, and the author of forgiveness is Jesus.[15]

TODAY'S ALONGSIDE PRACTICE

For today's practice, I want you to picture Jesus's face the moment the paralytic stood up.

What do you see?

Write it down here before you keep reading. If you're an artist, you could also draw how you picture Jesus's face.

For me, it's pretty clear. His face is soaking wet. It's covered in tears. Multiple times in Scripture we're told that Jesus cried (John 11:35; Luke 19:41; Hebrews 5:7–9). I'm convinced this is another one of those moments. And behind the saline, you know his face just beamed.

Most nights, before we tuck our kids in bed, we pray the priestly blessing over them from Numbers 6:24–26: "'The

Lord bless you and keep you; the Lord make his face shine on you and be gracious to you; the Lord turn his face toward you and give you peace.'"

What do you think the words *the Lord make his face shine on you*, mean? Have you ever walked into a room and seen someone who was so excited to see you that their face lit up? That's their face shining upon you. When God looks at you, his face glows with gladness. His gut reaction when his eyes meet yours is not judgment and condemnation, but love and compassion. The face of God toward you is one of delight.

Take a few minutes and try to memorize the verse below.

The Lord your God is with you, the Mighty Warrior who saves. He will take great delight in you; in his love he will no longer rebuke you, but will rejoice over you with singing. (Zephaniah 3:17)

SONG

"The Blessing" by Kari Jobe

DAY 3: JESUS REJOICES

"I tell you that in the same way there will be more rejoicing in heaven over one sinner who repents than over ninety-nine righteous persons who do not need to repent." (Luke 15:7)

QUESTION
Have you ever wondered what makes Jesus smile?

SCRIPTURE
My favorite chapter in the entire Bible is Luke 15. It starts out with some tax collectors and sinners gathered around Jesus. Then the Pharisees begin complaining about who Jesus is eating dinner with. And then Jesus does one of his favorite things: He tells some stories. Three of them. The first is about a shepherd who loses one of his sheep. The next is about a woman who misplaces a coin. And the last story is about a dad who loses both of his sons, each in different ways. But Jesus is a much better storyteller than I am, so turn to Luke 15:1–32 and do the wonder exercise for each of the three stories.

My Wonderings:
- I wonder how bad the younger son smelled when his dad embraced him?

- I wonder . . .

- I wonder . . .

- I wonder . . .

- I wonder . . .

- I wonder . . .

In order to answer our initial question about what makes Jesus smile, let's focus on verses 7, 10, and 21–24. Notice anything they have in common?

Repentance leads to rejoicing and celebration.

- ". . . there will be more rejoicing in heaven over one sinner who repents than over ninety-nine righteous persons who do not need to repent" (Luke 15:7).

- ". . . there is rejoicing in the presence of the angels of God over one sinner who repents" (v. 10).

- "Let's have a feast and celebrate. For this son of mine was dead and is alive again; he was lost and is found.' So they began to celebrate" (vv. 23b–24).

Repentance is doing exactly what the younger son did. After we've run away, it's turning around and coming home. It's making a U-turn. It's a change of heart, a change of mind, and a change of behavior.

STORY

Right after college, I was driving through Nashville with a girl I was trying to impress. In an unfamiliar town, I missed the road where I was supposed to turn and had to do the ever-dreaded backtracking. In my nervousness, I made an illegal U-turn and ended up getting pulled over by a police officer and slapped with a moving violation. It cost me a hundred bucks, a few cool points, and a lot of pride. U-turns can be intimidating on the road, but even more terrifying in real life. Especially when it involves admitting that we've been going the wrong way.

But in actuality, repentance isn't something we need to be afraid of. It never leads us to fear or regret. It invites us into a place of true refreshment.

When Peter was preaching in Acts 3, here's what he said about repentance:

> Repent, then, and turn to God, so that your sins may be wiped out, that times of refreshing may come from the Lord, and that he may send the Messiah, who has been appointed for you—even Jesus. (Acts 3:19–20)

> Another translation puts it this way: "Now you must repent and turn to God so that your sins may be wiped out, **that time after time your souls may know the refreshment that comes from the presence of God.** Then he will send you Jesus. . . ." (PHILLIPS)

In the original language, the Greek word translated *refreshment* actually means "a recovery of breath" or "to begin breathing easy."

There are two ways we typically run away from God. Both of them leave us breathless.

1. The first is when we make decisions like the younger prodigal son. When we choose to rebel and run after the false promises of the world. Typically, this leads to us trying to hide our guilt and shame. Trying to disguise the mess we've made. The cover-up takes a lot of work, and usually leaves us feeling anxious and breathless.

2. The second way we run away from God is similar to the older prodigal son. And the Pharisees. We try to earn his love with our own goodness. And it usually leads us

to a place of arrogance, independence, judgement and bitterness. Living like we don't need the grace of God is exhausting and will often leave us feeling breathless.

JESUS

How do we begin breathing easy again? How do we experience true refreshment? How do we enter into the rejoicing and celebration of Jesus?

We repent.

Not just one time, but multiple times, every day. **We live our lives in a pattern of death and resurrection.** It's the same pattern that Jesus talks about in the story of the lost sons. The Father says, ". . . this son of mine was dead and is alive again" (Luke 15:24a).

Remind you of anyone? **It's the pattern of Jesus.**

When life feels like it's hit a dead end, because of Jesus, we always have an invitation to make that U-turn. Paul writes in 2 Corinthians 5:17, "Therefore, if anyone is in Christ, he is a new creation. The old has passed away; behold, the new has come" (ESV). We don't have to keep eating the slop in the pig trough. We don't have to stay dead. We're invited to daily die and rise with Christ.[16]

A chapter prior, in 2 Corinthians 4:10, Paul writes, "We always carry around in our body the death of Jesus, so that the life of Jesus may also be revealed in our body."

The story of the prodigal sons is our story. But we're not one-time runaways. Running for us is an everyday event. We are constantly leaving our Father's house and returning. We're always dying and rising with Jesus. It won't be long after you close this book that you're going to mess up again. You're going to do things you promised you'd never do. Your mind is going to wander into dangerous territory. Your heart will search for someone else's affection, and sometimes return broken. Your body might get carried away with desires and sometimes come back home with scars. It might feel like you've gone through a type of death.

When that happens, don't run toward shame; run toward Jesus. Nothing makes him smile like a lost child running back home. When you fall down, allow Jesus to raise you to life again. That's actually how you grow in your relationship with him. That's how you begin to hear and recognize his voice. You learn how to live out this pattern of death and resurrection.

Jesus says, "For whoever wants to save their life will lose it, but whoever loses their life for me will save it" (Luke 9:24).

There are two primary ways we can experience dying to self.

1. By voluntarily surrendering our rights
2. By involuntary suffering[17]

Voluntarily surrendering our rights is similar to what we talked about last week on the foot-washing day. It's an intentional choice to die to self. To surrender. To sacrifice our time, money, gifts, and pride in order to put others above ourselves. When you give up an extra hour of sleep in the morning in order to help hold babies in the nursery at your church, you're voluntarily dying to self. When you spend time with an elderly widow, instead of binge watching a show, you're surrendering your rights. While these things can feel like big sacrifices, we do them with joyful hearts, trusting the promises of Jesus. He has shown us that death leads to resurrection and that we find life when we give it away.

Another way we experience dying to self is through involuntary suffering. There are many things you will go through in your life that are completely out of your control. Things that will be incredibly hard and things you didn't choose.

Maybe you've had one of your parents change jobs and, in turn, your family has moved away from all your friends. Maybe your parents' marriage died and there was nothing you could do to fix it. Maybe you had a family member or close friend gets seriously sick or even pass away. These are things we don't often understand, but they are opportunities for us to die and rise with Jesus. Many times, we're left wondering: *How can God bring good from this?* And sometimes we might never discover the answer to that question. But we can trust that God is always good and always working out his perfect plans for our good and for his glory. And while we don't always understand it, we can trust that he is a God who still raises the dead and is making all things new.

Today's Alongside Practice

Our repentance makes Jesus rejoice and leads us to refreshment. When we die to self, we are raised to new life. One difficult way to die to self is to confess your sin to God *and* to someone else. James 5:16a says, "Therefore confess your sins to each other and pray for each other so that you may be healed."

If you want to experience that healing and to be able to breathe easy again, confess your sin to a trusted friend. It wasn't until my freshman year of college that I confessed my darkest sins to anyone other than God. I still remember the moment it happened. I was in a Bible study with some other freshmen guys and we were meeting in the basement of one of our leaders' houses. We listened to a short talk about the concept of confession and then the small group time began. All lips were zipped. My heart felt like it was going to explode. Finally, I started confessing. And then crying. And then I waited. Terrified. Would these guys I'd only known for a couple months reject me? Would they judge me? Would they break my trust? To my surprise, my confession started a domino effect and each guy went around the circle. My new friends shared secret sins they'd been holding in for months and years. It's one of those nights I've bookmarked in my memory bank. Those friends now live in five different states, but for the past twenty-five years, we still have annually gathered together to play, to remember God's faithfulness, to pray for one another, and to confess our sin. Few things in my life have offered me greater healing and refreshment.

Would you be willing to ask the Lord to give you the courage to confess your sin to someone else? Maybe it's your Alongsider, a pastor, a Young Life leader, a parent, a sibling, or a friend. There is great power is bringing the darkness into the light. And your repentant heart will make Jesus smile.

SONG

"Grace Came Running" by 10,000 Fathers, Jon Jones, and Dee Wilson

DAY 4: JESUS WANTS

"When Jesus heard this, he was amazed at him, and turning to the crowd following him, he said, 'I tell you, I have not found such great faith even in Israel'" (Luke 7:9).

QUESTION

Yesterday, we talked about what makes Jesus smile. On our final day of this devo, let's look at one last question together: *What amazes Jesus?*

My childhood pastor, Dr. Gary Chapman, wrote one of the best-selling books of all-time called *The Five Love Languages*. The book explains how to best care for those you love by speaking their love language. Some people appreciate words of affirmation. My wife feels most loved by quality time. I love when others do acts of service for me. Others value physical touch or receiving gifts. I'm convinced that Jesus has a love language too. It's faith. He is most amazed, and feels the most loved by us when we demonstrate absolute trust in him. Jesus moves toward us with love, and we move toward him with faith.

There are hundreds of verses in the Scriptures that point to this reality, but one particularly makes me pause. In all of the Gospels, there is only one place where Jesus is recorded as being amazed. And the person who amazed Jesus happened to be a Roman soldier.

[Jesus] was not far from the house when the centurion sent friends to say to him: "Lord, don't trouble yourself, for I do not deserve to have you come under my roof. That is why I did not even consider myself worthy to come to you. But say the word, and my servant will be healed. For I myself am a man under authority, with soldiers under me. I tell this one, 'Go,' and he goes; and that one, 'Come,' and he comes. I say to my servant, 'Do this,' and he does it." When Jesus heard this, he was amazed at him, and turning to the crowd following him, he said, "I tell you, I have not found such great faith even in Israel." (Luke 7:6–9)

When we display faith in the midst of our fear, it makes Jesus marvel. Remember what happened when Jesus saw faith displayed in our gospel reading from Day Two of this week?

When Jesus **saw their faith**, he said, "Friend, your sins are forgiven." (Luke 5:20)

And then he made a paralyzed man walk. Jesus loves it when we put our unbridled trust in him.

SCRIPTURE

For our final gospel passage, open your Bible to Matthew 14:22–32 and give your imagination one last whirl.

My Wonderings:
- I wonder if the other disciples thought Peter was arrogant . . .

- I wonder . . .

- I wonder . . .

- I wonder . . .

Once again, the disciples find themselves in the midst of another storm on the Sea of Galilee.[18] Jesus had gone up on the mountainside to pray. When he looked down, he saw the disciples in the middle of their predicament. Since the boys had left Jesus without a boat, he took a little walk on the water. Of course, he could do that because he's the one who made the lake he was walking on. But as he approached, the disciples were taken off guard. They weren't expecting to see anyone walking on the water in the midst of a storm, in the middle of the night. But Jesus often shows up when and where we least expect it. And like the disciples, I often find him in nature.

Peter, the daredevil disciple, thinks he recognizes Jesus's voice. "Lord, if it's you, tell me to come to you on the water." Can you picture Pete slowly stepping out of the boat? Have you ever been on a high ropes course or climbed up a high diving board to jump off, and no matter what mental tricks you tried, you just couldn't keep your legs from shaking? I imagine Peter was feeling some slight vibrations in both his nerves and knees. With his white knuckles gripping the side of the boat, he lifted one leg over the edge and lost a sandal in the water. Like the waves around him, he kept going back and forth in his mind, debating if he was going to put his whole weight in the water.

Maybe that's how you feel when you think about trusting Jesus. Everything in you wants to do it. You know an incredible adventure awaits. You know Jesus has promised to give you abundant life to the full (John 10:10). But there's also a downpour of doubts filling your head like a sinking ship. The winds of fear feel full force in your face. When we look at the world, we will always have reason to doubt. Sin is real. Sickness is real. Hatred and evil surround us. But Jesus invites Peter, and you and me, to look beyond all of that into the reality of Christ's kingdom on earth. A kingdom where the king walks on water. A reality where King Jesus makes paralytics run. A place not ruled by hopelessness and death, but by a Risen King who makes all things new.

Peter had encountered this king, and in this history-making moment, he placed his trust in him. He became the first person, other than Jesus, to ever walk on water. And here we are twenty centuries later talking about him. Why? Because of his faith.

But that courage didn't last long. "When he saw the wind, he was afraid and, beginning to sink, cried out, 'Lord, save me!'" (Matthew 14:30).

The same thing is going to happen to you. One minute you're going to listen to the voice of Jesus and the next minute you'll turn up the volume on fear. And like Peter, you'll sink, too. It's that rhythm of death and resurrection we talked about yesterday. But look what happens when we fall down.

> But when [Peter] saw the wind, he was afraid and, beginning to sink, cried out, "Lord, save me!" Immediately Jesus reached out his hand and caught him. (vv. 30–31a)

Jesus

This is Jesus. This is the God-man we've been walking alongside over the last month. He's the One who loves you so much that every time you fall down, his gut response is rescue. He immediately reaches out his arms to hold you. One of my favorite songs is called "The Gospel." The bridge repeats these words over and over: *Oh, the arms of love fly faster than I can fall. Oh, the arms of love, they're in this room, holding us.*[19]

Who else loves you like that? Who else would you trust with your life?

After Jesus caught Peter, I wonder if he embraced him on the water. I wonder if Peter looked into eyes. If he did, I'm sure he encountered an overwhelming combination of compassion and strength. And then I imagine that the half-soaked disciple climbed back into the boat and fell to his knees.

> And when they climbed into the boat, the wind died down. Then those who were in the boat worshiped him, saying, "Truly you are the Son of God." (vv. 32–33)

This is exactly what happens when you're desperate for a rescue and you encounter a Savior. Your hope turns to faith. And your faith turns into worship.

As you continue on this journey of walking alongside Jesus, you might be tempted to earn his love. Or at least pay him back. And that typically either leads to a lot of guilt or a lot of pride. Instead, as you try to figure out what Jesus wants you to do next, listen to how Jesus answers the crowd when they ask him a similar question.

> Then they asked him, 'What must we do to do the works God requires?'
> Jesus answered, **"The work of God is this: to believe in the one he has sent."** (John 6:28–29)

The work of God is believing in Jesus. There's nothing more important for you to do.

If you want to know what Jesus wants, it's pretty clear. It's for you to believe in him.

I hope that over the past month, you've encountered the living person of Jesus. The one who walks alongside you every single day. As we wrap up this devotional together, my closing prayer for you comes from Paul's letter to the church in Ephesus. If you're able, would you read it aloud?

I pray that out of his glorious riches he may strengthen you with power through his Spirit in your inner being, so that Christ may dwell in your hearts through faith. And I pray that you, being rooted and established in love, may have power, together with all the Lord's holy people, to grasp how wide and long and high and deep is the love of Christ, and to know this love that surpasses knowledge—that you may be filled to the measure of all the fullness of God. Now to him who is able to do immeasurably more than all we ask or imagine, according to his power that is at work within us, to him be glory in the church and in Christ Jesus throughout all generations, for ever and ever! Amen. (Ephesians 3:16–21)

TODAY'S ALONGSIDE PRACTICE

When my wife and I were in seminary, we encountered many more trials than we were used to. One day we were listening to the hymn, "Come Thou Fount". In the second verse it says,

> Here I raise my Ebenezer;
> Hither by Thy great help I've come;
> And I hope, by Thy good pleasure,
> Safely to arrive at home.
> Jesus sought me when a stranger,
> Wandering from the fold of God;
> He, to rescue me from danger,
> Interposed His precious blood.
> (Robert Robinson)

I looked up the meaning of *Ebenezer* and discovered it meant "stone of help". In the Old Testament, in 1 Samuel 7, Samuel built an altar out of rocks and called it an Ebenezer. He built it as a reminder for the Israelites of God's faithfulness.

Natalie and I decided to create our own Ebenezer. We bought a big bulletin board and hung it on the wall of our den.

We covered it with sticky notes and pictures that reminded us of the countless ways God had helped us.

For this final Alongside Practice, you're invited to create your own Ebenezer.

- Maybe it's a list you make in your journal of ways God has answered your prayers and been faithful
- Maybe it's simply a page full of sentences that begin "Thank you Jesus for . . ."
- Maybe you want to get your own bulletin board or make your own project
- Maybe it's covering your bathroom mirror in Bible verses to remind you that God can be trusted

In Mark 9:14–29, there's an account of a dad bringing his demon-possessed son to Jesus.

The father says to Jesus, ". . . if you can do anything, take pity on us and help us."

Jesus questions the man's doubtful approach, "If you can"?

Then the Son of God replies, "Everything is possible for one who believes."

Immediately the boy's father exclaimed, "I do believe; help me overcome my unbelief!"

If you need a prayer to pray today, and every day, that's a good one to borrow. It's worth writing out with a dry-erase marker on your mirror.

"Jesus, I believe; help me overcome my unbelief!"

SONG

"Just As Good" by Chris Renzema and Ellie Holcomb

THE WEEKEND CONVERSATION

Below is a set of questions for you to talk through with your Alongsider this weekend.

1. Which day stuck out to you the most and why?

   ❏ Jesus Hates

   ❏ Jesus Forgives

   ❏ Jesus Rejoices

   ❏ Jesus Wants

2. Which gospel story most resonates with your own life?

   ❏ Jesus's crucifixion in John 18–19

   ❏ Jesus forgiving the paralytic in Luke 5

   ❏ The Prodigal Son in Luke 15

   ❏ Peter walking on water in Matthew 14

3. Share a few of your wonderings.

4. Which of the Alongside Practices did you enjoy most? Which helped you connect with Jesus?

   ❏ Reflecting on your sin and entering into a time of confession

   ❏ Picturing the face of Jesus

   ❏ Memorizing Zephaniah 3:17

   ❏ Listening to "The Blessing" song

❏ Confessing sin to another person

❏ Creating an Ebenezer

5. Why do you think those specific practices resonated with you?

• Had you ever thought about hating sin before?

• Was it hard for you to picture Jesus's face? What did you see?

• Have you memorized Scripture before? Do you still remember Zephaniah 3:17?

• Did you listen to the song, "The Blessing"? What were your thoughts?

• Have you confessed your sin to another person? If not, are you willing to try?

• Have you created an Ebenezer?

6. Which song did you most resonate with?

❏ "Lord Jesus, Comfort Me (A Communion Hymn)" by Matthew Smith

❏ "The Blessing" by Kari Jobe

❏ "Grace Came Running" by 10,000 Fathers, Jon Jones, and Dee Wilson

❐ "Just as Good" by Chris Renzema and Ellie Holcomb

7. Are there any ways you're understanding Jesus differently since you started reading the Alongside Devo?

8. How was your heart changed?

9. How can I be praying for you?

10. Discuss with your Alongsider what comes next. (Read the following pages to get some ideas of how to continue the conversation.)

WHAT'S NEXT?

Way to go! You did it. You made it all the way through *Alongside Jesus*!

But now what?

Below are three suggestions to keep it going:

1. CONTINUE TO WONDER THROUGH THE GOSPELS.

By now, you've learned how to engage the Scriptures through **IMAGINATION**. But we've only explored a handful of the amazing stories in the Gospels. Consider picking one of the four gospel accounts (Matthew, Mark, Luke, or John) and read the whole book slowly. As you read each day, continue grabbing your **JOURNAL** and sharing your **WONDERINGS**. How cool would it be to have a journal filled with hundreds of things you wonder about in the Gospels?!

In the final pages of this book, I've laid out a reading plan that takes you *slowly* through all four gospels over the next year and a half. Each day's reading is typically between 5–15 verses. And each week is laid out the same as this devo, with only four assigned readings per week. That's intentional. It's designed so that you can go slower and deeper and not get stressed out if you miss a day or two (or three) each week!

2. CONTINUE YOUR ALONGSIDE PRACTICES.

Throughout this devo, you've experienced more than twenty different **SPIRITUAL PRACTICES**—everything from

JOURNALING to **WALKING** to **WATCHING MOVIE CLIPS**. I've listed many of them below. Each day, after your gospel reading, consider engaging in one these practices, or get creative and come up with your own:

1. Listen to songs that help you focus on Jesus
2. Answer Jesus's *"Do you want to get well?"* question and share where you need healing
3. Hear someone else's story
4. Share your M&M's with someone
5. Make a list of things that distract you
6. Pray Psalm 51
7. Watch clips from *The Chosen* or the entire series (it's free online)
8. Watch meaningful movies or movie clips—like the one from *Les Misérables* (ask a trusted adult if they have any recommendations)
9. Fast from something
10. Rewrite your own version of the Lord's Prayer
11. Take a walk with Jesus
12. Ask your parents questions to try and understand them better
13. Journal
14. Imaginative Prayer (picture Jesus with you when you're anxious)
15. Secret acts of service
16. Reflect on and confess your sin to God
17. Picture the face of Jesus
18. Memorize Scripture verses and passages (like Zephaniah 3:17)
19. Confess your sin to another person
20. Create an Ebenezer

3. CONTINUE WALKING ALONGSIDE YOUR ALONGSIDER.

My guess is that one of your favorite parts of this experience has been the **CONVERSATIONS** you've had with your Alongsider. Why not keep that going? Even if you can't meet every week, could you have a fifteen-minute **PHONE CALL** and discuss what you're reading and hearing from Jesus? You could use these eight questions below for your ongoing weekend conversations:

1. What was encouraging about your week?

2. What was challenging?

3. Which gospel readings stuck out to you and why?

4. What are some of your wonderings?

5. Which Alongside Practices did you engage in this week, and did they resonate with you?

6. How are you understanding Jesus differently after this week?

7. How has your heart changed?

8. How can I pray for you?

And let us consider how we may spur one another on toward love and good deeds, not giving up meeting together, as some are in the habit of doing, but encouraging one another—and all the more as you see the Day approaching. (Hebrews 10:24–25)

LET'S CONNECT

My name is Drew and if we've never met, I hope we get to someday soon. I'm married to my best friend, Natalie, and we live in Greensboro, NC with our five kids, ranging from toddlers to teenagers. Their names are Honey, Hutch, Macy Heart, Hobs and Huddle.

If you want to connect, I'm on social media as @DrewHillNC.

You can also go to our website, AlongsideResources.com. There, you can find more resources to help you connect with Jesus.

I wrote a book similar to this for adults. It's called *Alongside: Loving Teenagers with the Gospel.* If you think it could be helpful for your parents, youth leaders, Young Life leaders, or any adults in your life, you can invite them to check it out on AlongsideResources.com. Also, if this devotional has been helpful for you, please share it with your friends and on social media.

Gratefully,

GOSPEL READING PLAN

Below is a **SLOW** plan to read through the four Gospels in one and a half years. In year one (52 weeks), you go through Mark (18 weeks), John (14 weeks) and Luke (20 weeks). In the first half of year two, you can read through Matthew (26 weeks). Some days' readings will be more challenging than others. The meaning of the text might be confusing or hard to understand. That's OK. When you feel stuck, I suggest you do one of two things:

1. Skip the day's reading and don't think twice about it. Show yourself some grace. **THIS ISN'T A COMPETITION.**

2. Ask a trusted adult to help you understand. There's an amazing story about this that is recorded in the book of Acts, chapter 8, verses 26–38. Take a moment and flip there. Acts was another book written by Luke and it's the first book right after the four Gospels. After you read it, I bet you'll be more motivated to **ASK FOR HELP!**

Remember as you read that you're not just reading a history book. God's Word is alive. Jesus is alive. And he longs for you to hear him speak.

> The Word that God speaks is alive and active; it cuts more keenly than any two-edged sword: it strikes through to the place where soul and spirit meet, to the innermost intimacies of a man's being: it exposes the very thoughts and motives of a man's heart."
> (Hebrews 4:12–13 PHILLIPS)

Year One: 52 Weeks (Mark/John/Luke)

Week 1
- Mark 1:1–8
- Mark 1:9–13
- Mark 1:14–28
- Mark 1:29–39

Week 2
- Mark 1:40–45
- Mark 2:1–12
- Mark 2:13–17
- Mark 2:18–22

Week 3
- Mark 2:23–28
- Mark 3:1–6
- Mark 3:7–12
- Mark 3:13–21

Week 4
- Mark 3:22–30
- Mark 3:31–35
- Mark 4:1–20
- Mark 4:21–25

Week 5
- Mark 4:26–34
- Mark 4:35–41
- Mark 5:1–20
- Mark 5:21–43

Week 6
- Mark 5:35–43
- Mark 6:1–6
- Mark 6:7–13
- Mark 6:14–29

Week 7
- Mark 6:30–44
- Mark 6:45–56
- Mark 7:1–13
- Mark 7:14–23

Week 8
- Mark 7:24–30
- Mark 7:31–37
- Mark 8:1–10
- Mark 8:11–21

Week 9
- Mark 8:22–26
- Mark 8:27–30
- Mark 8:31–9:1
- Mark 9:2–13

Week 10
- Mark 9:14–29
- Mark 9:30–37
- Mark 9:38–50
- Mark 10:1–12

Week 11
- Mark 10:13–16
- Mark 10:17–31
- Mark 10:32–34
- Mark 10:35–45

Week 12
- Mark 10:46–52
- Mark 11:1–11
- Mark 11:12–19
- Mark 11:20–26

Week 13
- Mark 11:27–33
- Mark 12:1–12
- Mark 12:13–17
- Mark 12:18–27

Week 14
- Mark 12:28–34
- Mark 12:35–40
- Mark 12:41–44
- Mark 13:1–13

Week 15
- Mark 13:14–23
- Mark 13:24–37
- Mark 14:1–11
- Mark 14:12–21

Week 16
- Mark 14:22–25
- Mark 14:26–42
- Mark 14:43–52
- Mark 14:53–65

Week 17
- Mark 14:66–72
- Mark 15:1–5
- Mark 15:6–15
- Mark 15:16–32

Week 18
- Mark 15:33–41
- Mark 15:42–46
- Mark 16:1–8
- Mark 16:9–20

Week 19
- John 1:1–4
- John 1:6–18
- John 1:19–28
- John 1:29–34

Week 20
- John 1:35–42
- John 1:43–50
- John 2:1–12
- John 2:13–25

Week 21
- John 3:1–15
- John 3:16–21
- John 3:22–36
- John 4:1–45

Week 22
- John 4:46–54
- John 5:1–18
- John 5:19–29
- John 5:30–47

Week 23
- John 6:1–15
- John 6:16–21
- John 6:22–59
- John 6:60–71

Week 24
- John 7:1–24
- John 7:25–36
- John 7:37–52
- John 8:1–30

Week 25
- John 8:31–59
- John 9:1–41
- John 10:1–21
- John 10:22–42

Week 26
- John 11:1–16
- John 11:17–37
- John 11:38–44
- John 11:45–57

Week 27
- John 12:1–11
- John 12:12–26
- John 12:27–50
- John 13:1–20

Week 28
- John 13:21–30
- John 13:31–38
- John 14:1–14
- John 14:15–31

Week 29
- John 15:1–17
- John 15:18–27
- John 16:1–24
- John 16:25–33

Week 30
- John 17:1–26
- John 18:1–14
- John 18:15–27
- John 18:28–40

Week 31
- John 19:1–16
- John 19:17–30
- John 19:31–42
- John 20:1–10

Week 32
- John 20:11–23
- John 20:24–31
- John 21:1–14
- John 21:15–25

Week 33
- Luke 1:1–25
- Luke 1:26–38
- Luke 1:39–56
- Luke 1:57–80

Week 34
- Luke 2:1–14
- Luke 2:15–21
- Luke 2:22–40
- Luke 2:41–52

Week 35
- Luke 3:1–38
- Luke 4:1–13
- Luke 4:14–30
- Luke 4:31–44

Week 36
- Luke 5:1–11
- Luke 5:12–16
- Luke 5:17–26
- Luke 5:27–32

Week 37
- Luke 5:33–39
- Luke 6:1–11
- Luke 6:12–26
- Luke 6:27–36

Week 38
- Luke 6:37–49
- Luke 7:1–10
- Luke 7:11–17
- Luke 7:18–35

Week 39
- Luke 7:36–50
- Luke 8:1–18
- Luke 8:19–21
- Luke 8:22–25

Week 40
- Luke 8:26–39
- Luke 8:40–56
- Luke 9:1–17
- Luke 9:18–27

Week 41
- Luke 9:28–36
- Luke 9:37–43
- Luke 9:44–56
- Luke 9:57–62

Week 42
- Luke 10:1–24
- Luke 10:25–37
- Luke 10:38–42
- Luke 11:1–13

Week 43
- Luke 11:14–28
- Luke 11:29–36
- Luke 11:37–54
- Luke 12:1–13

Week 44
- Luke 12:14–21
- Luke 12:22–34
- Luke 12:35–48
- Luke 12:49–59

Week 45
- Luke 13:1–21
- Luke 13:22–35
- Luke 14:1–24
- Luke 14:25–35

Week 46
- Luke 15:1–32
- Luke 16:1–18
- Luke 16:19–31
- Luke 17:1–19

Week 47
- Luke 17:20–37
- Luke 18:1–8
- Luke 18:9–18
- Luke 18:19–30

Week 48
- Luke 18:31–43
- Luke 19:1–10
- Luke 19:11–27
- Luke 19:28–44

Week 49
- Luke 19:45–48
- Luke 20:1–19
- Luke 20:20–47
- Luke 21:1–19

Week 50
- Luke 21:20–38
- Luke 22:1–30
- Luke 22:31–46
- Luke 22:47–53

Week 51
- Luke 22:54–71
- Luke 23:1–25
- Luke 23:26–43
- Luke 23:44–49

Week 52
- Luke 23:50–56
- Luke 24:1–12
- Luke 24:13–35
- Luke 24:36–53

Year Two: Matthew (26 weeks)

Week 1
- Matthew 1:1–17
- Matthew 1:18–25
- Matthew 2:1–12
- Matthew 2:13–23

Week 2
- Matthew 3:1–17
- Matthew 4:1–11
- Matthew 4:12–25
- Matthew 5:1–12

Week 3
- Matthew 5:13–16
- Matthew 5:17–20
- Matthew 5:21–26
- Matthew 5:27–32

Week 4
- Matthew 5:33–48
- Matthew 6:1–4
- Matthew 6:5–15
- Matthew 6:16–18

Week 5
- Matthew 6:19–24
- Matthew 6:25–34
- Matthew 7:1–6
- Matthew 7:7–14

Week 6
- Matthew 7:15–29
- Matthew 8:1–4
- Matthew 8:5–13
- Matthew 8:14–17

Week 7
- Matthew 8:18–22
- Matthew 8:23–27
- Matthew 8:28–34
- Matthew 9:1–8

Week 8
- Matthew 9:9–13
- Matthew 9:14–17
- Matthew 9:18–26
- Matthew 9:27–34

Week 9
- Matthew 9:35–38
- Matthew 10:1–15
- Matthew 10:16–25
- Matthew 10:26–42

Week 10
- Matthew 11:1–19
- Matthew 11:20–30
- Matthew 12:1–14
- Matthew 12:15–21

Week 11
- Matthew 12:22–37
- Matthew 12:38–45
- Matthew 12:46–49
- Matthew 13:1–23

Week 12
- Matthew 13:24–30
- Matthew 13:31–35
- Matthew 13:36–43
- Matthew 13:44–52

Week 13
- Matthew 13:53–58
- Matthew 14:1–12
- Matthew 14:13–21
- Matthew 14:22–36

Week 14
- Matthew 15:1–20
- Matthew 15:21–28
- Matthew 15:29–39
- Matthew 16:1–4

Week 15

- Matthew 16:5–12
- Matthew 16:13–20
- Matthew 16:21–28
- Matthew 17:1–13

Week 16

- Matthew 17:14–21
- Matthew 17:22–27
- Matthew 18:1–5
- Matthew 18:6–9

Week 17

- Matthew 18:10–14
- Matthew 18:15–20
- Matthew 18:21–35
- Matthew 19:1–12

Week 18

- Matthew 19:13–30
- Matthew 20:1–16
- Matthew 20:17–28
- Matthew 20:29–34

Week 19

- Matthew 21:1–11
- Matthew 21:12–17
- Matthew 21:18–22
- Matthew 21:23–32

Week 20

- Matthew 21:33–46
- Matthew 22:1–14
- Matthew 22:15–22
- Matthew 22:23–33

Week 21

- Matthew 22:34–40
- Matthew 22:41–46
- Matthew 23:1–12
- Matthew 23:13–39

Week 22

- Matthew 24:1–14
- Matthew 24:15–35
- Matthew 24:36–51
- Matthew 25:1–13

Week 23

- Matthew 25:14–30
- Matthew 25:31–46
- Matthew 26:1–13
- Matthew 26:14–30

Week 24

- Matthew 26:31–46
- Matthew 26:47–56
- Matthew 26:57–68
- Matthew 26:69–75

Week 25

- Matthew 27:1–10
- Matthew 27:11–26
- Matthew 27:27–31
- Matthew 27:32–44

Week 26

- Matthew 27:45–56
- Matthew 27:57–66
- Matthew 28:1–15
- Matthew 28:16–20

ENDNOTES

1. John Freeman, Imagination Seminar (Greensboro, 2017).

2. Victor Hugo, *Les Misérables: Tome 1* (Le Livre de Poche, Hachette, 2000).

3. Dane C. Ortlund, *Gentle and Lowly: The Heart of Christ for Sinners and Sufferers* (Wheaton: Crossway, 2020), 75.

4. https://www.motherjones.com/media/2012/06/supersize-biggest-sodas-mcdonalds-big-gulp-chart/

5. "St. Patrick Quotes (Author of the Confession of Saint Patrick)." Goodreads. December 9, 2021. https://www.goodreads.com/author/quotes/688258.St_Patrick.

6. Richard J. Foster, *Celebration of Discipline* (San Francisco: Harper One, 2018), 127.

7. "Brennan Manning Sermon: Kingdom Works 1999 Video." YouTube. YouTube, November 5, 2007. https://www.youtube.com/watch?v=QY7c6XPagmA&t=2s.

8. The movie is called *Courageous* (directed by Alex Kendrick; Sherwood Pictures, 2011), and I know people who love it and others who don't. This is not an endorsement to see it, but if you search YouTube for "Courageous opening scene," it's pretty powerful.

9. Idea borrowed from my friend, David Page.

10. Idea borrowed from my friend, Steve Chesney

11. Idea borrowed from pastor Tim Keller

12. *The Book of Common Prayer* (New York: The Church Hymnal Corporation, 1979), 331.

13. "To Be a Christian: An Anglican Catechism" Question #107

14. Ibid. #108

15. I believe I heard this first said by the late Doug Coe in a conversation.

16. Idea introduced to me by my friend, Elijah Lovejoy.

17. Idea introduced to me by my friend, Elijah Lovejoy.

18. If you're struggling to believe that any of this is true, go on YouTube and search videos for "storm on the Sea of Galilee." There are tons of recent videos that people have posted when they've been by the Sea of Galilee during a storm. Sometimes seeing it in real life can help it move from feeling like a fairy tale to something that actually did occur 2,000 years ago.

19. Jonathan and Melissa Hesler, "The Gospel" *Beautiful Surrender*, Bethel Music, 2016.